*Lucky Joe's Namesake*

# LUCKY JOE'S NAMESAKE

*The Extraordinary Life and Observations of*

## JOE WILSON

Edited by Fred Bartenstein

With a Foreword by Barry Bergey

**CHARLES K. WOLFE MUSIC SERIES**

Ted Olson, series editor

The University of Tennessee Press

*Knoxville*

The Charles K. Wolfe Music Series was launched in honor of the late Charles K. Wolfe (1943–2006), whose pioneering work in the study of American vernacular music brought a deepened understanding of a wide range of American music to a worldwide audience. In recognition of Dr. Wolfe's approach to music scholarship, the series will include books that investigate genres of folk and popular music as broadly as possible.

*First Edition.*

Names: Wilson, Joe, 1938–2015. | Bartenstein, Fred, 1950– editor.
Title: Lucky Joe's namesake: the extraordinary life and observations of Joe Wilson / edited by Fred Bartenstein; with a foreword by Barry Bergey.
Description: First edition. | Knoxville: The University of Tennessee Press, [2017] |
Series: Charles K. Wolfe music series | Includes bibliographical references and index.
Identifiers: LCCN 2016049352 (print) | LCCN 2017006965 (ebook) |
ISBN 9781621903161 (pbk.) | ISBN 9781621903253 (pdf)
Subjects: LCSH: Wilson, Joe, 1938-2015.
| Folklorists—United States—Biography. | Folk music—United States.
| Folklore—United States. | United States—Social life and customs.
Classification: LCC GR55.W57 A25 2017 (print) |
LCC GR55.W57 (ebook) | DDC 398.092 [B] —dc23
LC record available at https://lccn.loc.gov/2016049352

Joseph T. Wilson
March 16, 1938–May 17, 2015

"Lucky Joe" Wilson was a Tennessee mountaineer who fought with the Union army, fell in with "vicious associates," stole horses, and rose from the dead in a North Carolina jail cell. His namesake great-grandson led an equally exciting life: from a voracious reader in a two-room mountain school, to the early country music scene in Nashville, to the front lines of Birmingham's civil rights struggles, to Madison Avenue consulting, to directorship of the National Folk Festival and National Council for the Traditional Arts.

## "LUCKY JOE" WILSON

*Episodes in the Career of a North Carolina Horse Thief*

WELDON, N.C. March 8.—"Free, thank God!" was the exclamation of "Lucky Joe" Wilson a day or two ago when he was discharged from the penitentiary. With other convicts he had worked on farms near this place.

"Lucky Joe" is a white man, and eight years and six months ago he was convicted in Yadkin County for horse stealing. While an appeal was pending, "Lucky Joe" grew sick in jail, and became worse until his life was despaired of. He was attended by the county doctor, who finally pronounced him dead.

He was prepared for burial and laid in a coffin. At night a light was put in the room, the door was locked, and the supposed corpse was left without watchers. The next day, when the Sheriff and his assistants went in to carry out the remains for interment, the casket was empty and "Lucky Joe" could not be found.

It was found that the supposed dead man was making tracks for Tennessee. Knowing that he would be pursued, "Lucky Joe" took another horse without leave of the owner in order to facilitate his escape. The feeling against him was so great that a plot was made to catch him and bring him back. His family resided in Ashe County, and after persistent watching of the mails he was run down in Tennessee. He was brought back and lodged in Yadkin County Jail.

His appeal was overruled and he was sentenced to ten years in the penitentiary. He had saved some money and made the most strenuous efforts to secure Executive clemency, but without avail. He served eight years and six months, and gained one year and six months by good behavior.

"Lucky Joe" served all through the war under Gen. Stoneman and was a brave and faithful soldier. His bad conduct after the war was due to vicious associates and excessive use of liquor. While in prison he made application for a pension, which was granted, with $4,000 back pay. This money he deposited in the savings bank at Raleigh, where it now is.

---

*The New York Times*, March 9, 1893

# CONTENTS

## CIVIL RIGHTS



## FOLKLORE AND FOLK FESTIVALS



## THE CROOKED ROAD



## MISCELLANY

# ILLUSTRATIONS

# FOREWORD

Joseph T. "Joe" Wilson was the great-grandson of "Lucky Joe" Wilson, a hard-drinking, horse-stealing Civil War veteran who in 1884, according to one account, escaped from his coffin and the custody of the sheriff to return to his homeland in the remote mountains of East Tennessee.

The twentieth-century Joe Wilson led a life that was as improbable—but not nearly as ignoble—as that of his namesake. For him, the journey started when his family's beloved but aged work horses were about to be sold. Realizing that life on the hill country farm would never be the same, he hitchhiked to Nashville, arriving during the florescence of commercial country music.

Subsequently, his professional path wound through Civil Rights-era Birmingham and the fundraising and financial offices of Madison Avenue before settling him for twenty-eight years near the seats of power in our nation's capital as the executive director of the National Council for the Traditional Arts (NCTA). In that role, he developed a national model for folk festival presentation, stalked the halls of federal offices on behalf of traditional artists, and filled the halls of concert venues with audiences eager to experience the work of master folk musicians. Along the way, he became a powerful advocate and engaging writer on behalf of agrarian values, social justice, artistic authenticity, and cultural democracy.

This volume, a companion to *Roots Music in America: Collected Writings of Joe Wilson* (also published by the University of Tennessee Press), brings us Wilson's life and observations, mostly in his own words. I'm convinced that Joe is the only person on this earth equipped with the wit and storytelling skills to adequately narrate that saga. As Julia Olin, his successor as executive director of the NCTA, has said: "Joe wrote like he talked and talked like he wrote." In a colloquial style that echoes some of Wilson's homegrown literary heroes—H.L. Mencken, Mark Twain,

Abraham Lincoln, and Will Rogers—these pieces reflect what it was like to spend a chunk of time with Joe.

A visit with Joe was always intellectually peripatetic and emotionally invigorating. Discussions were interwoven with the playing of recordings you just had to hear, suggestions of books and articles you really should read, and the recounting of obscure historical and cultural facts that you ought to know. All of this was served up with a friendly smile, a sparkling eye, and an infectious enthusiasm that left you awed, amused, enlightened, and sometimes exhausted—Joe could outlast almost anyone when it came to conversation.

I first met Joe in 1976 when, as the new director of the NCTA, he came to St. Louis to try to talk the Missouri Friends of the Folk Arts into hosting the National Folk Festival in the town where it originated in 1934. He arrived wearing a polyester suit that was slightly unkempt and of a color not found in nature. It was accessorized with a boldly patterned, haphazardly knotted, free-range tie splayed across his torso. We didn't know what to make of him at first. Was he a backwoods savant, a door-to-door salesman, a musical promoter, or an eccentric escapee from academe? It turned out that he was a little bit of each.

Joe immediately took an interest in what we were doing in Missouri, encouraging us to continue documenting traditional musicians in the Ozark region. He returned time and time again to help us mount a festival on the grounds of the Gateway Arch, in concert with the National Park Service, and he prodded us to apply for grants from the National Endowment for the Arts (NEA) and the National Endowment for the Humanities (NEH).

He loved to join us on recording trips, because he was deeply interested in the artists and their work. Joe also loved fiddling with the equipment, all the while professing the unique qualities of Neumann microphones and Revox recording machines: "Son, those mics are so sensitive they can pick up the sound of a chigger grittin' its teeth out in the yard." It is not surprising that over the course of his career Joe was responsible for the documentation of numerous musicians and musical groups, as well as the production of hundreds of recordings of artists previously unknown to the general public.

As was the case in Missouri, folklorists around the country knew Joe to be both a force of nature and a force of nurture. If you were fortunate enough to be linked to the Wilson-wide-web, you surfed waters that were broad, deep, and sometimes unpredictable. He once attended a conference in Utah and encountered Sally Haueter, a precocious young folklore student who had a particular interest in traditional arts. On the spot, and much to his supportive (and, may I say, patient) wife Kathy James's surprise, Joe invited Sally to come to Washington, D.C. and intern at the NCTA. It was left to Kathy to reassure the new mentee's parents that there were no ulterior motives in this offer, to ready their home for a guest, and to arrange for long-term housing. As Kathy—whose attention to Joe's health undoubtedly extended his life by many years—once commented: "It wasn't always easy to live with Joe, but God was it interesting."

Joe's work at the NCTA set a standard for the field of folklore. Advocating for intensive fieldwork, equitable representation, and responsible presentation of traditional arts and artists, he re-initiated the practice of moving the National Folk Festival around the country, leaving a legacy of ongoing and successful annual events in cities that included Lowell, Massachusetts; East Lansing, Michigan; Bangor, Maine; Richmond, Virginia; and Butte, Montana. Through NCTA, and with NEA funding, Joe initiated domestic tours featuring culturally specific musical traditions, including Irish American, Mexican American, Franco-American, Jewish, Ozark, Cowboy, African American, and Native American artists. He also devised tours that highlighted the diversity of our nation's artistic excellence, such as *Masters of the Steel String Guitar, Masters of the Folk Violin, Masters of the Banjo*, and *Saturday Night and Sunday Morning.*

He had a long-standing and special relationship with the National Endowment for the Arts. When my predecessor Bess Lomax Hawes became the director of folk arts at the NEA in 1977, she found a powerful ally in Joe Wilson. He was involved in discussions with senior agency staff when a freestanding folk arts program was but a gleam in Bess's eye. Joe worked with her to develop a network of folk arts expertise around the country. He conceived of the idea of touring under-represented traditional artists to under-served communities. When the case for the value of governmental support of folk arts—and indeed for the importance of federal support of arts programs in general—needed to be made to the broader public or on Capitol Hill, Joe was the first to volunteer both his services and his opinions.

When the NEA National Heritage Fellowship Program was initiated in 1982, the NCTA took on the production of the ceremonies and celebratory events. I remember a story that Bess told about one of her experiences with Joe. In the second year of the program, honorees included Ray and Stanley Hicks, who lived on Beech Mountain in North Carolina, not far from where Joe grew up. Ray was a master storyteller and Stanley, his double first cousin, was an instrument maker, musician, and dancer. Three days before the ceremony and concert, Bess learned that the two really didn't care to make the trip to Washington, D.C. Knowing that Joe had close connections with both of them, she enlisted him to convince them to reconsider. Bess and Joe flew to Bristol, Tennessee, rented a car, drove out to their cabins, and chauffeured them to the events accompanied by non-stop stories and song. I heard both Bess and Joe say that this was the best road trip of their long and productive careers.

Joe's broad knowledge of folk arts helped to shape White House cultural events, public television and radio programming, and presidential inaugural celebrations. U.S. cultural diplomacy efforts were shaped, in part, by Joe's work with the United States Information Agency and its Arts America program. His impact on U.S. cultural policy also included lobbying for the creation of the American Folklife Center at the Library of Congress. His advocacy in the halls of Congress insured that the National Park Service and other agencies gave culturally diverse and geographically dispersed artists and their communities the requisite degree of attention and support.

In later years, his importance to the field was acknowledged through a variety of honors, including a Living Legend award from the Library of Congress and a National Heritage Fellowship from the National Endowment for the Arts.

Joe was motivated by a deep sense of moral accountability and an even deeper faith in our capacity to right wrongs—if we only tried hard enough. He was a self-described skeptic but an intellectual and religious polymath. I can remember him saying something to the effect that he was Baptist by music, Catholic by visual arts, Quaker by behavior, and Unitarian by belief. In matters related to equity and justice, he was a voice for the unheard, a limner of the unseen, and a champion of the under-appreciated. During his days in Birmingham covering the civil rights movement, Joe wrote about injustices he witnessed. As the chapter on Birmingham in his autobiographical essay attests, Joe did more than observe and describe—he also several times put his body on the line.

Joe played a significant role in the careers of a long list of performers through the years. He first encountered and worked with Marty Robbins in Nashville, following that fateful journey from the farm. Later, musicians such as Doc Watson, Ricky Skaggs, Jerry Douglas, Alison Krauss, John Cephas, Michael Doucet, Seamus Connolly, John Jackson, and D.L. Menard—to name just a few—benefited from Joe's friendship and support. Thanks to Joe, many of these performers were booked during the early stages of their careers on international tours representing American culture to overseas audiences.

Joe Wilson deeply cared about the artists who embody our cultural heritage. Lesser-known traditional artists could find no greater friend than Joe, and his commitment extended well beyond their expressive lives. Dee Hicks, who would not have been heard via the popular media, was a national treasure and a walking library of centuries-old ballads. In 1977, Dee and his wife Delta, who had never traveled far from the Cumberland Plateau in Tennessee, attended the National Folk Festival in Vienna, Virginia. They returned to their home to find that it had burned to the ground. Joe quickly mobilized a group of NCTA board members and, within days, raised enough money to purchase a new place for them to live.

It was Joe who first came up with the idea of selling CDs of traditional artists through the gift shops of the Cracker Barrel restaurant chain. He produced and wrote the liner notes for an inaugural series on the Cracker Barrel label that was so successful that eventually the corporation contracted with Gaylord Entertainment, owners of WSM and the Grand Ole Opry, to continue the label. In what could be viewed as an ironic and circular twist of fate given his early foray to Nashville, Joe's contribution to one of the most successful strategies for distributing commercial country recordings is largely unknown and unacknowledged today.

As this collection demonstrates, Joe's talent as a storyteller is based on his ability to convince us that we are starting from common ground. He once opened a conversation with our five-year-old son with the comment: "I was five years old once—for a whole year." His tales most often invite us to meet him at a certain place and at a particular time. When we join him there, we may be in southwestern Virginia or northeastern Asia, and the time could be post-Civil War or pre-Civil Rights. From that point on, the craft of a master tale-teller transports us to the destination he has chosen.

Though he spoke softly and with a relaxed cadence, Joe was no stranger to rhetorical sword fights, and the ingenuity of his verbal repartee was suitable for a Shakespearean play set on a Tennessee mountainside. I recall him describing someone as so low that "wearing a top hat he could easily slide undetected under the belly of a snake." Voicing his concern for accurately representing Appalachian musical traditions in public presentations, he once stated that "you can't squirt a little vinegar on a cucumber and call it a pickle." Joe clearly enjoyed the back and forth of it all and expected to get as well as he gave. He did know when to let up though. After months of skewering a political operative whose views he found particularly objectionable, word came out that the target of Joe's disdain was suffering from a terminal illness. Joe held fire and responded with, "When God puts his hand on somebody, I take mine off."

With regard to fate and mortality, Joe certainly lived up to his namesake's lucky moniker. Over the time that I knew him, he survived two kidney transplants, heart surgery, and ongoing diabetes, among other issues. A fall from a ladder injured his heel and put him on crutches for a good while. Afterward, he told me that if you ever have the choice between landing on your head or your heel, choose your head. And then there was the near beheading. One evening, Joe was driving along Sligo Creek Parkway near his Maryland home. An unsecured gate used for closing the road swung onto the hood of his car, crashed through the windshield, knocked off his headrest, and emerged from the rear driver-side window. After hearing the story, a disbelieving friend mentioned that he could have been killed, and Joe responded, "I'm cheating the Devil every day."

In his final years, Joe retraced that fork in the road he took early in life and turned toward home. Although he left the farm, the farm never really left him. He and Kathy relocated to the little milling town of Fries in southwestern Virginia and, although technically retired, he found new ways to tell the story of his region, which in many ways was his story.

Joe developed and later directed the Blue Ridge Music Center near Galax, Virginia, and his voice can still be heard narrating the videos in its interpretive exhibition. He also conceived of and named The Crooked Road: Virginia's Heritage Music Trail, writing the *Guide to the Crooked Road* and putting together the recordings that accompany that publication. In the dedication prefacing that guide, he says of the musicians of southwestern Virginia: "Among the lessons they teach is that an art form that is freely given and always shared can be kept forever." This book shares Joe's lessons and artful ruminations culled from a lifetime of cultural and social activism. As readers, we are ultimately the lucky ones.

BARRY BERGEY
*Bethesda, Maryland*

# PREFACE

It was 1972. I was twenty-one and a college student in Massachusetts when I first edited Joe Wilson's writing. He was thirty-four and a New York-based fundraiser, indulging—as a moonlighter—his gift for writing and his love for the roots music he grew up with in Tennessee. I published "Bristol's WCYB: Early Bluegrass Turf" in *Muleskinner News,* which I edited from 1969 to 1974. I believe he sent the piece unsolicited. Two years later, we commissioned and ran his stellar Doc Watson profile. (Both of these articles are included in the companion volume, *Roots Music in America: Collected Writings of Joe Wilson.*)

Fast-forward a decade and a half. I was living in Ohio when Joe started bringing National Council for the Traditional Arts concert tours, such as *Masters of the Folk Violin* and *Masters of the Banjo,* to Dayton for the local arts organization, Cityfolk. Joe and I were delighted to encounter each other again. We subsequently worked together to bring the National Folk Festival to Dayton (1996–1998) and on strategic planning for The Crooked Road: Virginia's Heritage Music Trail (2006). Joe contributed the foreword to *The Bluegrass Hall of Fame: Inductee Biographies 1991–2014,* which I co-wrote and edited for the International Bluegrass Music Museum.

Editing Joe again after so many years and experiences triggered a brainstorm. It would be fun to assemble a book-length anthology filled with Joe Wilson's brilliant published writing for magazines, concert program books, and album liner notes, along with his sizzling online posts, letters to the editor, and privately circulated unpublished writing. I phoned Joe, left a voicemail, and he called back a few days later full of enthusiasm. That same day (October 10, 2014), waves of e-mail attachments and brown envelopes began to barrage my mailboxes. Joe's wife, Kathy James, said the project energized him like nothing else, as a series of health challenges sapped his strength, constrained his travels, and led to his untimely death on May 17, 2015.

Soon, Joe's many friends caught wind of the anthology venture and began to suggest must-include pieces, including incendiary personal correspondence. Since Joe had grown up in Tennessee, and because the University of Tennessee Press had a series named for Joe's friend and collaborator Charles K. Wolfe (1943–2006), I approached Ted Olson and Thomas Wells at the press. After letters of support from folk music scholars Neil Rosenberg, Howard Sacks, and David Whisnant, the publisher enthusiastically jumped on board.

The more I worked with Joe's material, the clearer it became that it called for *two* books: a collection of pieces on roots music (the subject on which he was most prolific), and a volume focused on Joe's extraordinary life and eclectic observations. I decided to title the second volume *Lucky Joe's Namesake,* because the story of Joe's "badass" great-grandfather (see p. vii) was so compelling, and because of how much Joe identified with Lucky Joe (his email address started with "LuckyJoe38").

*Lucky Joe's Namesake* needed as its centerpiece an extended autobiographical essay, which Joe had never written. But he had been interviewed numerous times between 1979 and 2015, and his storytelling skills made him a dream interview subject. His friends helped me unearth three long unpublished interviews and oral histories, including essential material on Joe's less-documented civil rights years. From these transcripts, five published interviews, and emails from Joe, I was able to construct a reasonably coherent narrative (see pp. 3–47), adding to Joe's words some non-substantive connective tissue and a few bracketed explanations. This process, undertaken posthumously, omits topics that I would have liked to include, such as Joe's adult family life and his work as a New York consultant. Joe would certainly have covered those subjects had his interviewers asked about them, or had he lived to write or collaborate in a true autobiography.

In the last eight months of his life, Joe was intensely involved in selecting material and reviewing my edits for the anthologies. After his passing, the decisions were mine, although I received valuable input from Joe's friends and associates, and from early readers in my own circle.

Several editing issues are worthy of comment:

1) Joe regularly recycled content for his various writing projects, often with revisions, cuts, and expansions. In preparing the anthologies, I tried to use his most colorful and complete language, even if that meant drawing upon more than one source for a single article. Conversely, I removed duplications whenever the same or similar material appeared in original versions of several articles.
2) In editing the two volumes, I tightened and occasionally resequenced Joe's prose for clarity's sake, and because, in the format of an anthology, some of his extended tangents—such as "Minstrelsy (Or Why Blacks Gave up the Banjo)" (included in *Roots Music in America*)—could have their own article.
3) Mark Twain famously said, "Never let the truth stand in the way of a good story, unless you can't think of anything better." Joe was a consummate storyteller. Wherever I could correct his facts without damaging his story, I did so. Although we had a few arguments about matters of historical accuracy, Joe usually came around in the face of confirming evidence. I'm not aware of any egregious misstatements in these volumes, but I did not painstakingly check every one of Joe's facts. Joe's family and friends suspect a few places where he stretched elements of his personal story for literary effect. We decided to leave these in, because we liked them as well as Joe did. Joe appreciated the discipline of folklore, considered himself an amateur folklorist, and would have both understood and loved the process by which his life underwent the transformation to legend. Joe wasn't above hastening that process along.
4) Joe had many talents, but filing and archival preservation were not among them. His papers were kept in piles whose order wasn't entirely clear to him, and when he did find something he was looking for, it was usually to lend it to someone who may not have gotten around to returning it. When he changed computers, many of his old files failed to make the transition. In his last years, he adamantly recalled pieces he had once written, with just enough clues to send me, Kathy, and friendly research librarians on wild goose chases that snagged some of the articles in this volume. I'm sure there's more great Joe Wilson writing out there, but I don't know where to find it.

Kathy told me that Joe's retirement plans included writing several books on historical topics. He wanted to author a volume on Virginia's Great Road (articles in both *Roots Music in America in America* and *Lucky Joe's Namesake* contain early results of that research). She urged him to write a book on the origin stories of well-known songs and tunes. "The Wild Horse at Stony Point, with a Salute to Peter Francisco and a Bow to Jenny Lind"; "Rachel and the Eighth of January"; and "Durang's Dance and Hoffmaster's Tune" in *Roots Music* are samples of how that book would have turned out. But in retirement Joe lacked the stamina and the access to research associates that such major projects would have required.

Joe Wilson spent the bulk of his life and energy as a doer and a change agent, and the country and world are much the better for it. It is fortunate that his considerable talents as a writer and scholar found sufficient expression to leave a published legacy. I am proud to have made a contribution to that enterprise, and thoroughly enjoyed my time of intimacy with Joe's extraordinary voice.

FRED BARTENSTEIN
*Yellow Springs, Ohio*

# ACKNOWLEDGMENTS

Many people and organizations helped in the preparation of this volume of Joe Wilson's writings. First among them, of course, is Joe Wilson himself. He spent seventy-four years amassing the experiences and observations contained here; in his last eight months, he was a most enthusiastic collaborator.

I received valuable input from early readers, including Joy Bartenstein, Richard Brown, Carolyn Fuller, George Holt, Kathy James, Mary Mathews, Elaine Morris Roberts, Neil Rosenberg, Howard and Judy Sacks, Richard Spottswood, and Andy Wallace. In addition to writing the Foreword, Barry Bergey gave most helpful advice in shaping the project.

A number of sources generously granted permission for the reprint and revision of pieces that originally appeared elsewhere. They include the American Folklife Center at the Library of Congress, Jan Arnow, Betty Belanus, Birmingham Civil Rights Institute Oral History Project, *Bluegrass Unlimited,* the Center for Southern Folklore, The Crooked Road: Virginia's Heritage Music Trail, Mark Lynn Ferguson, *Folklore Forum,* Carolyn Fuller, Sandra Gutridge Harris, Jack Hinshelwood, Kathy James, Johnson County [Tennessee] Historical Society, Ken Landreth, Jon Lohman, the National Council for the Traditional Arts, *Old-Time Herald, The Progressive,* the Publore Listserv, Neil Rosenberg, *Sing Out!, Smoky Mountain Living,* Eugenia Snyder, StoryCorps, *The Tomahawk* (Mountain City, TN), The University of Tennessee Press, Andy Wallace, and a variety of personal correspondents. (Take just a moment to reflect on who other than Joe Wilson could have published in all those places!)

Denise Jarvinen, RaShae Jennings, and Kelly Skidmore generously transcribed interviews and oral histories. Research librarians Aaron Smithers at UNC Chapel Hill and Amy Margolin at the Greene County,

Ohio Public Library went beyond the call of duty in tracking down articles, sometimes with only the slightest of clues. Andy Wallace—Joe's long-time right-hand man at NCTA—was great about digging through files there, and Kathy James was indefatigable in chasing down paper, computer files, and photos in her and Joe's Fries, Virginia, home. Jack Hinshelwood, executive director of The Crooked Road; Jon Lohman, state folklorist of Virginia; and Ken Landreth, Joe's friend and neighbor, sent colorful correspondence included in the "Joe's Gems" section. Charley Pennell provided the index.

# AN EXTRAORDINARY LIFE

# Growing Up in the Blue Ridge (1938–1956)

I come at this from the fringes. I was born March 16, 1938, at Creston, Ashe County, North Carolina, on a piece of land that my mama inherited from her pappy, who had inherited it from his pappy. It's on the Tennessee/Virginia line, at the top of the Blue Ridge on the upper reaches of the New River at what is called the head of the river, the beginning of the New River. The New River is the oldest river in North America; it rises on Snake Mountain just above where I was born and flows north across Virginia and West Virginia to the Ohio River. All the old rivers flow north: the Nile and the New and several others.

My mother's family, the Sutherlands, had been there since the colonial period, so when my father and mother were married, my father borrowed $100 from my grandmother—his mother-in-law—and built a two-room house out of chestnut scrap lumber. Both my older brother and I were born there; I've got an older brother [Kenneth], a younger brother [James Walter], and a younger sister [Julia].

A few years later—I was very small—we moved across the state line six or seven miles to Trade, Tennessee, where my father's family had been since the colonial period. The Trading Ground is there. You find the earliest mention of the Trading Ground in William Byrd's book, *The History of the Dividing Line*, written in 1728. It's the dividing line between North Carolina and Virginia—the colonial line. Byrd mentions pack traders coming from eastern Virginia to the mountains to trade with Indians, but Indians had traded there long before anyone else came. As I grew up there, anytime we plowed, we would find obsidian that'd been brought there and traded because it made good points.

At the time that I grew up, Trade was still fairly remote. Johnson County, Tennessee, is the state's easternmost county, right up in the tip. There was one two-lane road that had been paved for a few years that trailed through there, full of hairpin turns. Trade was a place too small to have a crossroad; the best we could do was a T-road [see the collection of articles on Trade, Tennessee, at the beginning on page 51].

## CHILD LABORER ON A TENNESSEE FARM

My father was a farmer and a postmaster, at one point. He bought and sold and traded and lived by his wits, like everybody else there. We had a farm, and our agriculture was much like agriculture in the late 1800s elsewhere in the country. We grew our own food: vegetables and so forth, and raised our own animals. We had a cash crop: tobacco, that we grew there. We also grew some vegetables to sell: snap beans, green beans, some strawberries. Tomatoes grew very well there. We grew some grain crops: wheat and oats, and my father was still cutting them with a finger cradle, a thing that goes back to biblical times. But mainly it was tobacco and cattle.

I got started in work when I was six years old. I was the water boy, and from then on I had a job on the farm. The leisure of childhood hadn't quite reached the Appalachians when I was being raised.

I couldn't have been more than seven or eight years old, and we were building a barn. A white man from nearby Mountain City, Tennessee, came to help lay the concrete foundation, bringing with him three black hired hands. Partway through the morning, the white man asked my mother, "Well, when it comes to eating, what are we doing?"

She said, "We'll all eat together."

"No. No," the man told her, as if she'd suggested the impossible. "Can't eat together!"

Without missing a beat, my mother motioned toward the black workers: "Well, that's the hardest work there is to be done, so if they're going to eat separate, I'll feed them first." We ended up all eating together, and it was just fine.

When I was a little guy, there was one black farmer who lived near us. My father told me about the threshing crew going past him and not taking care of him. I asked him why, and he said it was because he was black. And that didn't make sense. I remember that as my first sense of injustice.

You know, the mountains never had many blacks. Johnson County people didn't have slaves, and black people didn't move there after the Civil War. My county at one point was the most Republican county in the United States. When Alf Landon ran against Roosevelt in 1936, they voted eighty-six percent for him. Now, I'm not saying the people there were not racist. Being racist got spread around real well, you know.

Hell, up there they were all Yankees in the Civil War, too. The "Mountain Yankee" Cavalry group walked the mountaintops from behind the Confederate lines to join the Union army. I have a picture of my great-grandfather, Joseph T. ("Lucky Joe") Wilson, in his Civil War "Mountain Yankee" uniform. He was sixteen when he joined up. He was in Company I (mainly men and boys from Trade and Shouns, the next town over) when they raided into Greenville, Tennessee, in 1864 and killed the famous "Kentucky Raider," Confederate General John H. Morgan. He became so famous for badassery that people were still telling "Lucky Joe" stories when I came along, a generation after he died. His fame as a badass was so widespread that a North Carolina tobacco manufacturing company named a form of plug tobacco for him.

We worked Morgan horses on the farm. I was good friends with the horses, and my brother and I would ride them in the mountains on Sunday. We'd plow out tobacco with a little cultivator, and they knew not to step on the tobacco plants. We also used them in the woods, because we had a little peckerwoods sawmill business. I learned how to pull the handle of that saw and stay out of the way, because there'd be something go by your head at ninety miles an hour—a nail somebody had put into a tree years ago or maybe just a knot—but enough to send you to see Jesus.

## MOUNTAIN MUSIC LEGACY

My father sang gospel in quartets. My mother knew old songs, ballads, and older country things. So there is some music on both sides of the family. My uncle Will on my mother's side played guitar, had a rack-mounted harmonica, and knew some nice songs. My uncle Alf on my father's side loved the fiddle; he wasn't a great player, but he was engrossed with it. Uncle Willet—a neighbor, not a relative, who lived up the road—played the banjo. When I was a little guy, they would play and I thought that was glorious. I was so small that I was sitting under the table. I can remember the feet of the musicians and the sounds of their instruments—it's one of my earliest memories.

My great-aunt Sally—my grandfather's sister—played an old wood banjo, an Appalachian banjo, unfretted and a groundhog skin top on it with a maple body. There are lots of those around where I'm from. Aunt Sally's father, "Lucky Joe" Wilson, taught her to play the banjo, and she said he was a fine singer. Aunt Sally would play the banjo on the back porch and sing old ballads. She's the only person I know of who ever played one of those things on the radio. She had a fifteen-minute radio program weekly on WOPI in Bristol as "Carolina Sally," singing on the Saturday afternoon jamboree.

So, yes, I grew up in the Tennessee mountain culture and loved it from the beginning. I liked the music, and I liked the people. I liked the dance, the crafts, and all of the things that were there. When I learned that there was music like this in other cultures, I found that I liked that too.

## TWO-ROOM SCHOOL AND THE BOOKMOBILE

I went to a two-teacher school two miles up a dirt road. Those schools were like those of the 1800s; we had outhouses, tree swings, and all kinds of things of that sort. The teachers there had not been to college; they had graduated from high school and taken a "how to teach" course. They were local women and they were fine, but they had four grades, each of them—twenty-five kids in a room. That's a considerable task, so those overworked women had jobs for each child. We had a big stove and I built the fires there.

When I was in the third grade, my teacher let me keep the library, which was a bookcase. The bookmobile came every six weeks from East

Tennessee State. I got to pick the books and check them in and out, so I thought that I had to read them all because it was my job to keep them. I did that from the third grade until the eighth grade.

I was such an avid reader that the bookmobile people liked me, so they would drop books off for me in the summer. I was reading sometimes 300 books a year. No one guided my reading much—I was all over the map. When I was in the seventh and eighth grade, I became interested in archaeology, so I read everything I could about Egypt. Just read about Egypt for years and years, and all the early anthropology. No one other than me paid much attention to my reading. When I got to high school, they didn't know what to do with someone who liked books as much as I did; there were no SAT tests.

If I had to name one thing that was really important in setting me on my path in life, I would say it was the bookmobile. The holiest place on earth to me is that place in Alexandria in Egypt where the ancient library stood. I've never been there, but I intend to go sometime.

## REFINING MUSICAL TASTES

I think I was twelve years old when I learned chords on a guitar. The social milieu of the music the way I first heard it was around houses—people visiting and so forth—and of course in church, which was a very different kind of music, and at pie suppers at country schoolhouses. The first thing I ever saw that amounted to anything like a performance was at a country high school.

I always preferred live performance and still do. If anybody played in the area, I usually went to see them, and usually I didn't pay. I was very adept at getting in without paying—waited until the guy turned his back and went through the window, you know. I started going to fiddlers' conventions in the early fifties—slipped off and went to them. I went to both the Galax [Virginia] and Union Grove [North Carolina] conventions in 1952, when I was fourteen.

I listened a lot to WCYB in Bristol, that station and a lot of others. WJHL, Johnson City, did a thing called *Barrel of Fun*. WPAQ at Mount Airy, North Carolina, was another favorite, and of course the Grand Ole Opry on WSM. There were also Lowell Blanchard's programs out of Knoxville, WWVA, WRVA from Richmond, and—believe it or not—the

Texas border stations you could get clear as a bell at night. There was Fran Russell at WCYB; he was also the guy who put on the *Farm and Fun Time* thing. There was Cousin Don McGraw from WOPI in Bristol. I can remember Nelson King from Cincinnati, Randy Blake from Chicago.

I became much more discriminating about what I liked then. I have to say a little more eclectic too, because up until that time, I hadn't liked anything except old-time music and country that was real solidly country. I can't even say that I liked western swing at that point, until I saw the Miller Brothers and decided that I did like that music. The people that I knew of and liked the most were the fiddlers and banjo players: Wade Mainer, Flatt and Scruggs, and Bill Monroe.

I didn't have a record player and I couldn't afford the records. In fact, I suspect if I'd bought a record player, I probably never would have played any music, which might have been a blessing for the few people who've heard me play.

About '52, when I was in high school, we formed a little band [The Country Cousins] which had a two-fingered banjo player, a biscuit-board steel guitar, a guitar, a mandolin, and a fiddle. Sort of a typical band of that time, and we did what typical bands of that time did. We weren't worth a whole hell of a lot, and I was the least of the bunch. I played a little bass, I knew some chords on the guitar, I sang some, and I tend to be able to tell when things are in tune. Actually my job was keeping the thing organized—that was what I turned out to be best at.

It was near the end of the radio era, but we went over to the radio station at Boone [North Carolina] and played there on Saturdays. If you could stand it through our broadcast, Doc Watson came on after we did—and he was just as good then as he was later. I think we were on radio before I ever realized that music attracted some of the dear young ladies. I am not sure that we ever had a set of groupies, but we came damn close. It took me until I was about eighteen or nineteen to realize I could never be a good guitarist. I quit playing at that point.

## HIGH SCHOOL SKEPTIC

For some reason, I became a religious skeptic. When I was about twelve years old I'd been to one of those revival meetings where they preached everybody right into the middle of hell, which was real hot and went on forever. I thought, "That's mean. I'm not that mean. Only an eternal fiend could build an eternal hell." And the thought went through my little hillbilly head: "This is all a sack of crap!" I waited for the lightning to hit me, but it didn't.

The preachers were all preaching against Charles Darwin—"Man didn't come from a monkey," you know. I wanted to read Mr. Darwin's book. It was hard as hell to get that book in East Tennessee in the forties, but one of the gals who worked on the bookmobile liked me, so she indulged my wish to read Charles Darwin. I read it through, turned it over, and read it through again! And it made a lot of sense—but that was kind of a scandal.

One of my high school teachers said, "Show me proof that Charles Darwin was right. I don't want to go to the South Seas, or any islands, or any of that. Show me proof right here in Johnson County." And I said, "Well, see that rail fence over there on the hill? Look at the blackberry briars growing along that fence. A blackberry is actually a cluster of seeds. There's a luscious sweet thing around each little tiny seed. The bird eats those off, and he goes over and he sits on the rail, and he poops. The fertilizer that comes out of his cloaca, along with the seed, lands in this rotting log down there. So you have all this bunch of blackberry vines and what you're looking at here is the blackberry briar manipulating the bird." He looks at me a while and he says, "You're crazier than hell, but I'm gonna leave you alone."

There was one high school in the county, and it was in Mountain City; Trade is about eleven miles out. When I got there, kids were listening to rock. One of the things that is hard for outsiders to realize is that—in those counties—places like Mountain City are kind of uptown. The bigger schools are near town, and you have a different kind of kid there. They are not farm kids like us, not from up the hollows. At that point, a kid who grew up in Mountain City was remarkably like a kid from a burb outside of Rochester. The music with depth tends to be out a little further. That's not to say there aren't people in town who play and listen to it, but I can't remember a good fiddler from the Mountain City area who actually lived in Mountain City.

I graduated from Johnson County High School in '56. I don't know why they didn't desegregate it. That county didn't have enough black folks to hold a first-class funeral. They were old-line families who had always been there, and they could've desegregated it with no trouble at all, but no one did; no one moved quick. I guess that part of the country was preoccupied with other kinds of things.

I came along at a time when—all over the country—there was this great shift of rural people to urban places, and a consolidation of farms. These things have continued; they're still going on, and all of the stress of farm people that you see now, it really goes back to then.

Staying on an Appalachian farm was not really an option when I grew up. There were 105 people in my graduating class, and three years later there were only five or six of them left in the county. There wasn't anything to do in the rural areas, so I joined the mass exodus.

# Learning about Life (1956–1959)

In 1956, at age seventeen, I took to the road with my dad's last twenty dollars in my pocket and my right thumb in the air. There have always been a lot of mountain people who came to Washington, D.C., and that's where I first went. I had friends there and people I knew. You know which city in the country, over a twenty-year period from the '50s up into the '70s, received the highest number of Appalachian migrants? Washington, with Atlanta second. Much of demography gets ignored. People guess at it and they get the wrong guesses.

## WORK AND MUSIC IN WASHINGTON

I did anything that I could do. I worked for a little while at Cohen's Quality Shop, a little clothing store on King Street in Alexandria. That lasted a couple of months; I got bored and moved over to the airport. Then I started just bumping jobs all around the area. I worked for the U.S. Geological Survey for a little while. And there, if you worked for someone for a week or two, that was long enough. So I was famous for, you know, walking in and staying around for a little time. I thought that was what you were supposed to do. I was just learning about life.

When I came to Washington, Jimmy Dean was working at 14th and W Streets at the Capitol Arena, where the Howington Brothers were also playing. Jimmy Dean was the headliner, and he always had Buck Ryan and Smitty Irvin do a couple of things on the fiddle and banjo. He had Billy Grammer play something on the tenor banjo too. The Stonemans were working at the Famous Club. Mac Wiseman was there a lot then. The Dixie Pig, which is somewhere out in Northeast, had some good music. Buzz Busby had a nice band. There was good bluegrass all around.

## HIGHER EDUCATION CALLS

Finally, after a couple of years, I saved enough money to go to Lees-McRae College in North Carolina. That is a little Presbyterian junior college; I think they charged $300 per semester tuition. I was working my way through, so I enrolled two weeks late, because I needed a little more money.

Our history professor—in History 101, which was world history—had started with the civilizations in the Tigris and Euphrates River valleys and the standard stuff about Egypt. He'd been teaching diligently for two weeks, and here's a schmuck who comes in two weeks late. So he gives a pop quiz that day, and our grade gets based on the pop quiz, so he makes some kind of sarcastic remark and then he writes three questions on the blackboard. And I look at them, and they're actually pretty simple questions. They were about things I knew about, so that was when the reading came in handy. I terribly impressed that fellow.

Between my freshman and sophomore years, I worked at Pep Boys [an auto parts chain] as a salesman. I could sell, so I made enough money to get through. I stayed at Lees-McRae for two years, which is the only higher education that I ever had in daytime. I did the rest in night school. I've been in more night schools than you would believe. From there, I went to night courses at the University of Tennessee at Nashville, University of Alabama—Birmingham Center, and Samford University. I did some things at Columbia when I was in New York. I never did get a BA, but I have enough hours.

At the time I was doing this, you had to spend a semester on campus to get a BA. Campus residence was a requirement. So at one point, I got a letter from the University of Alabama that said I could get a degree if I'd come to Tuscaloosa for six months. I never bothered to do that. I never met anyone who thought that a BA was worth six months in Tuscaloosa! Obviously there are people who do—because there are University of Alabama graduates, a lot of them every year—but not the people I met.

After a while, the degree didn't matter. I was interested in learning about things. The last person of authority who looked at my transcript said, "This is amazing!" going down through it. I have enough hours for a bachelor's in five or six different subjects, apparently. And I still take courses occasionally, because I recognize that education is a forever process.

## FORK IN THE ROAD

I worked the summer of 1959 in Ohio, hanging drywall for my brother who was in construction, and then I came down to Johnson City to go to East Tennessee State. I thought I could work out enough money in various jobs. So I got a job reading to this blind guy—he and I were friends—and it was one of several things that I was going to do, but I was $1,500 dollars short. It was the very early years of Pell grants, and I was able to tell Claiborne Pell himself later on that I didn't get one of his grants. The financial aid person said, "Anybody's family can come up with $1,500." But I didn't ask, because I knew they didn't have it, and I would only hurt their feelings. So I had to leave East Tennessee State.

On my way home, between Johnson City and Elizabethton, I realized that when I got up to our little farm the horses would come to meet me. We'd raised Fan, who was the older horse, from when she was a colt. She was the same age as my older brother, and then she had a colt, Bud, that I helped to raise. The boys—even my younger brother—had all left home and my dad had bought his first tractor, a Massey Ferguson. Dad liked the horses, but he couldn't afford to retire a horse. He had to sell those horses, and what you sold them to was the dog food place.

I knew I couldn't talk him out of it, and it wasn't fair to him and to my mom, but I didn't want to see my horse go down the road in the back of a truck headed for a dog food plant. That was just more than I could stand, so instead of coming home I went to Nashville.

I had always listened to the Grand Ole Opry and, like every other hillbilly kid, I loved all this music from there. I wanted to see some of it, and see if there was anything I could do.

# Nashville (1959–1962)

I drifted into Nashville in late '59 sometime. Country music recording was relatively new, and upcoming artists and writers were arriving there then. I made friends with some of them, including Willie Nelson, who was selling encyclopedias door to door to feed his songwriting habit. I haven't seen him in a while, but I understand that he no longer needs to sell encyclopedias [see "When Willie Came to Town" in *Roots Music in America*].

For the three years I was in Nashville, I attended night school at the University of Tennessee and hung around the music, listening and just enjoying it. I worked at other things, off and on, like covering car seats and an automotive warehouse. It was all piecework. I worked for Marty Robbins, who was a well-known country musician. I helped Marty build a micro-midget racetrack in Smyrna, Tennessee, and I helped on a couple of tours.

## BACKSTAGE AT THE OPRY

I went to the Grand Ole Opry so I could help Marty's steel man get his amps inside and get things set up. Vito [Pelletieri] kept track of all of the songs—who wrote them and who published them—so the Opry could pay off ASCAP and BMI [music licensing organizations]. At that point, I had a good memory and good knowledge of who wrote all those hillbilly songs—a better one than Vito—so I'd help him with that.

They only had one security guy backstage: Old Captain Norris, a retired Nashville policeman. He sat by the door that was on 5th Avenue and if somebody wanted to barge in, the captain would find out who they wanted to see and ask whether that person wanted to see them. One night, there was a bad drunk boy who wanted to come back there. He gave the old captain a shove, and the captain wasn't able to cope with this kid, who might have been nineteen or twenty and big. I remember that his chin stuck out; he looked like Dick Tracy in the cartoon. I got this urge to hit him, and I did, right on the end of that chin just, as hard as I could. He landed on his ass, and I had my clodhopper boots on—because I'd been working for Robbins out at the track—so I kicked him some. He said, "Let me leave, sir, let me leave!" He went crawling out, and I got a job.

The captain said, "I know you help Vito, but from here at the door you can hear everything on the stage. If you hang around here a little closer, I'll give you ten dollars." So between Vito and the captain I made thirty dollars every Saturday. Hell, that was more money than I was making the rest of the week!

## FRINGES OF THE RECORD BUSINESS

You couldn't make a living then doing any kind of freelance work in music. I could write a little bit—probably as well as the average Nashville liner note writer—and could do some photography and other things like that, but it was a scramble. I picked up custom jobs at a few of the studios. Most of the stuff that I worked on has never had a credit line on it, and thank God it is all out of print.

I liked the kind of music they were recording over at Starday Records, especially the "limited collectors editions" of bluegrass and older styles of country music. So I hung around there and picked off the crumbs. I helped to produce some of those godawful "twelve top tunes for $1.98" outrages where the record company would send $500 down from New York and you would get as few musicians as you could together—because you had to split the money—and do the whole album. You would start at like eight o'clock at night and try to have it finished by three or four the next morning. You would have a record player and listen to the hit record a few times and try to figure it out. We did "Polka on the Banjo," the Scruggs thing. Martin Haerle, who later went to CMH, was singing on that a little bit. Martin had a nice German accent at that time and you could hear, "Polka on zur banjo" on the chorus.

Don Pierce, the president at Starday, learned that there was a world of record buyers outside the South who would buy stuff like that. And he moved in to fill a virtual void. The small label business was nothing like it became in the sixties and particularly during the seventies. Most of the time I'm sure he didn't realize what he was dealing with, and if he had any sense of aesthetic at all I don't know where he kept it. But he got a lot of good stuff on wax that otherwise might not have been recorded.

Living by my wits—whatever needed to be done, I would do it. If it was a gospel record, I would write some kind of fluff about people I didn't know anything about—you know, "the good Christian songs of the American South." It was a great learning process. I can't say that the work I did was worth all that much.

Working around record studios is a good way to learn the breadth of music that exists. It is also a good way to learn to what lengths people's egos will push them to record bad things, and make great sacrifices to do it. It will teach you an appreciation for the talent of the session musician. The session musician learns to play—I think the phrase is—as little as he can as well as he can. You learn why that's necessary, with all of these uneven people coming in that you have to back up. And if you try to be any kind of sparkling thing, you will burn yourself out in a year or two.

It's a great way to learn how the commercial music world is organized. I'm glad I learned it. I'm not particularly interested in doing that kind of thing now [1979]. In fact I am almost repelled by the thing that Nashville is now, roughly the same set of aesthetics that General Motors uses in making hubcaps: "Will it sell? You stamp it out!"

Even then, Nashville didn't have any room for people like me; I was not cut from the same material. It was understood and accepted as gospel that the country music of Ernest Tubb and Lefty Frizzell and Hank Williams—though he was dead by then—needed to change. I went there right at the beginning of the crossover period. Presley had come up and recorded, and people suddenly realized that you didn't have to sell 10,000 copies of a record—you could sell a million if you just did this, this, and this.

There was a determination in the industry to make music that would be palatable to a huge percentage of the population. In order to do that, you added "doo-wah" choruses a la the Jordanaires—who were in tremendous use at that time—and the string section of the Nashville Symphony. You cut off all the sharp edges. You "packaged it."

Country music stopped being a rural music form. Above all, they wanted to get rid of those crude-sounding banjos and other acoustic instruments. They wanted to get rid of songs about mama dying and other emotional material that just scared the hell out of those middle class, plastic-eared people they wanted to sell to. But I happened to like those sharp edges that were being rounded off. I've always trusted my ears in my judgments about music, and my ears said that Flatt and Scruggs were great, and that Bill Monroe was just absolutely wonderful, and that their music and that of some of the other bluegrassers who were passing through then was the best music there.

I have to say that, as a business decision, I can't quarrel with what they did. It worked; country music's share of the market grew tremendously during that period. They were successful, and their job was to deal with the "demon that walks in the shiny black grooves," to quote John Hartford—that demon called commercial success. No one ever asked whether the music was good. No one ever asked if it was beautiful. They asked, "Will it sell?" and if the answer was "yes," then it was good and beautiful. I began to feel very out of place.

## LUNCH COUNTER SIT-INS

I came of age during the civil rights period, and it seemed important to me to involve myself in some of that. In 1959 or thereabouts, I began to attend the Unitarian Church in Nashville. There were a bunch of other religious and political skeptics there, who were very aware of all of the things that were going on: the sit-ins and the bus boycotts. I was not a participant in any of those, but I knew about them. We'd had some difficulties when the State of Tennessee was trying to shut down the

Highlander Center, which was then at Monteagle. I remember meeting Guy Carawan there. He was into the music and could pick the guitar a little better than I could. We tried to make the state authorities ease up on them. [The Highlander Folk School, founded in 1932, provided training for labor and civil rights leaders. After the State of Tennessee closed the school in 1961, it moved to Knoxville as the Highlander Research and Education Center.]

About that time, they had the lunch counter sit-ins over in North Carolina. [The sit-ins were in Greensboro. The 75th National Folk Festival, held in 2015, included oral history sessions commemorating the events of 1960.] A group of kids in Nashville—from Tennessee State and Meharry Medical College—were going to try to desegregate some downtown lunch counters. We knew about that over at the Unitarian Church and were eager to help. I remember one planning meeting with John Lewis, a seminary student. He was not a Tennessee State guy, but James Bevel was and Diane Nash was; I remember meeting both of them.

The word went out that it would be good if some of us could go over and become regular customers at those places. When the sit-ins started, if they shut them down, we could be sitting there beating on the counters saying, "What are you closing down for, God damn it? We want to eat!" I was assigned to Harvey's, a major downtown department store. They'd had a contest to choose the best apple pie recipe—the "Million Dollar Pie"—and then they were going to serve it at their restaurant. I'd heard the advertising but I hadn't tried the pie. I liked apple pie. See, you were going to order the same thing every day and wear the same clothes, so they would get used to you as a regular customer.

The students kept putting off when they were going to do it, and I was eating a slice of that pie every day. At any rate, when the day came, the management didn't pay any attention to us as regular customers. They threw our ass out just like they did everybody else. I guess it was thirty years until I could eat apple pie again. I got sick of that stuff—the things you give up, trying to do good!

Though things were better for me in Nashville financially than they had ever been, there came a day when I decided to leave. And I did.

# Birmingham (1962–1966)

I went to Alabama in '62 and worked for the Iron and Steel Worker's Credit Union in Birmingham. I managed the credit union's student loan program, edited the organization's publication, and went to night school at the University of Alabama at Birmingham and Samford College. I wrote part-time, worked on some civil rights things, and was there for the "Battle of Birmingham." [The Southern Christian Leadership Council's Birmingham campaign of 1963 organized black college, high school, and elementary students to nonviolently confront civil authorities, resulting in changes to the city's segregation laws.] I did some work for the old *Southern Courier*, which was a civil rights paper at the time. And I did stringing for several newspapers and widely scattered news organizations. I did an article for *The Progressive* magazine [see "Hucksters of Hate—Nazi Style"] in which we tried to identify some of the Birmingham bombers.

It was exciting work for a while, but mainly there were just threatening circumstances. I was never hurt by anyone, but I had a great deal of invective and profanity aimed at me. And there were times when there were some bricks and some people pretending they were going to do me grave injury, but they didn't.

When I came down there, everybody knew that Birmingham was going to be tough. It had the reputation of being the most segregated city in the United States. Early '62 was before any real hell broke loose. Well, there'd been the bus boycotts, and there'd always been this set of the Klan in Birmingham. The National States Rights Party (NSRP) was in full bloom; they were all over the place. Every time you looked sideways, one of them came by with their Confederate regalia. Something was going to happen.

## FREELANCE JOURNALIST

One of the ways I'd made money to attend college was to write term papers for people, so I got to thinking of my writing skills as a way to make a little more money, and God knows I needed money. I sold some stuff to Reuters as a stringer; I think they were getting rewrite privileges from American newspapers, but they wanted somebody that had an eye on the thing. The Brits have always thought they could analyze and understand things better than Americans, but they wanted to be able to smell it and taste it as well.

I had two old Rolleiflex cameras—both two and a quarter by two and a quarter—that would shoot twelve pictures in a row. When I came down for the demonstrations, there were lots of reporters in Birmingham, writers who didn't have a camera or couldn't take a picture. They knew that I was getting out in front and taking some stuff, so I sold the film right out of the camera. I had slow film, so you could blow it up real big. I knew what each camera would do; one of them had a flash on it and one didn't. I started out at ten dollars a roll, got up to twenty, and made over a hundred dollars in one day. Hell, that was more than I was making in a week!

I remember one picture that I've only seen one time. Dr. King was leading a group of people across a viaduct. It was in the wintertime, and he had on an overcoat. The Chamber of Commerce had a dorky slogan: "It's nice to have you in Birmingham." It was on a billboard, with this dude waving a hand out of a nice family car, and here's Dr. King, quizzically looking sideways at it. I took that picture. I saw it in a French publication years and years ago.

I was developing my own pictures at home—more of a bathroom darkroom—but whoever bought that film took it to the developer and put his name (or his organization's name) on it. I always thought that I made a fair trade; they put their money on something that might've been nothing. They took their chance and I took mine, and that's fair.

## CONFRONTING SEGREGATIONISTS

My ex-wife Pat [Joe married the former Patricia Jean Deaver in 1961. Their children and their birth years are: Melinda (1963) and Laurie (1964). The couple divorced in 1983.] was the chairman or the president of this little organization called Public Education Peacefully. She and her friend Peggy Fuller were big activists. They were all out of the Unitarian Church. One time, after he was voted out of office [as Birmingham's Commissioner of Public Safety], Bull Connor came to a meeting where there was going to be a discussion of education, and he was talking too much. Peggy Fuller wheeled around to him and said, "Will you shut up?" He did, he shut up—"I'm sorry, ma'am."

Bull Connor was never as bad as people made him out to be. He was always a bigmouth—he had been a radio sports announcer; everybody in Birmingham listened to his broadcast—and that's really what he had going for him. He wanted to be the leader of the police, but when they did things that were—you know—slaughter, he didn't go for that. That was almost a tragic thing. He could just as easily have been a good man if he had stopped, or if somebody had been able to lay a hand on him and say, "Wait a minute, Eugene, shut the shit up and listen for a second. This is the way it's going to go, and you can be a hero here." But there was no person like that, and he got the hell beaten out of him by life, and he would go down in history as one of the miscreant jackasses that did incredible harm. [Connor's Birmingham police let Klansmen viciously beat Freedom Riders, employed dogs and fire hoses, and arrested more than 3,000 demonstrators, including 959 children.]

The loudest of the NSRP leaders was a fellow called David Stanley. He was from Canada, and there was a jackleg preacher who was associated with Texas, so lots of people who were caught up with them came from other places. The editor of their *Thunderbolt* magazine was this chiropractor, Edward Fields, and you could scrape hell and the bottom of the ocean and not find a slimier character.

But the really dangerous one was Jesse Stoner, who had been teaching bombing schools across the South for years. He was from Lookout Mountain up in Chattanooga, had gone to the McCallie School up there—fancy school—knew all the rich kids from all the rich families. He was a lame man who was crippled—and I'm not sure why, whether it was polio or what—but he was evil personified. He always wore a gray suit, had a little red bowtie in the best of shape, and always lived well. There was a Greek restaurant at Five Points West; he always ate there.

I watched him for a long time because I was, you know, kind of pushy in an odd way. I thought there were people who were supposed to know about all of this, and that was the FBI. They were all over the place in Birmingham, and we thought that they had everybody wiretapped. Whether they did or not, I'm not sure, but we thought—at least I thought—that they should have Jesse in a cage, that he was leading a lot of this.

So I went to the FBI and asked them. They knew about me because I was running the little talk group that met on Sunday evenings at the Unitarian Church. I went up and talked to the chief agent. I didn't get anything out of him, of course. I asked the guy something about Fields, and he happened to mention Stoner. I said, "He's a hell of a lot more dangerous than Fields," and that's the one time when he tipped his hand. He said, "You got that right." That was the only time he confirmed anything I said. It was a strange investigation they ran—they were so protective of everything. I must have a nice file over there.

Some of the NSRP guys were psychotics. You take a person like "Dynamite Bob" [Robert Edward Chambliss (1904–1985)]. There was a screw loose in Bob; he was crazy. If you went to an NSRP or a Ku Klux Klan thing, he was one of the enforcer types. He was out walking around, looking at everybody, and you know—funny enough—I think that son of a bitch knew who I was, but he didn't *really* know who I was. I think he thought I was one of them.

I think Bob was one of the four guys that were taking pictures of my friend and neighbor Ed Harris's house. Ed's kids were a little older than mine, maybe six or seven years old; my kids were toddlers. We were having black families—black parents—at our homes. I was standing on my porch one Sunday when that was going on, and I saw these four guys. They had cameras and they were taking pictures of the black folks coming and being greeted by the Harrises. They were doing it in a way that they didn't mind if you noticed—an attempted intimidation is what it was.

I had a pump shotgun, and I'd cut that barrel off just a quarter of an inch beyond the legal length. I loaded that sucker with birdshot and then buckshot—alternate loading. I'd taken the plug out to shoot eight times; I didn't have one in the chamber, because I had little kids. I walked out on my porch and jacked the load into that thing,"chk-uh." One of the guys taking pictures looked at me, and I could see the fear in his eyes even at that distance. It scared the bejesus out of him. It scared all of them, and he knew my name, because he said, "Mr. Wilson, we was just taking some pictures. We—we—we're through, we're gonna leave."

I said "We've got little children; we don't like having you around here. You might want to leave as fast as you can, because otherwise you might wind up asking St. Peter for the loan of an old gown." He didn't have any sense of humor—he didn't laugh at that. He says, "We're leaving, sir," and I walked them up the street into an alley where they had an Oldsmobile parked. It left there at a great rate of speed and peeled a little rubber, you know, and they didn't come back.

Maybe it's my imagination—it's been fifty years, and remembering how people looked over a span of that many years is a tricky business—but I thought then that one of them was Dynamite Bob. I think I scared him so damned bad that he'd forgot what I looked like. He could be scared—I know that—and I think basically those guys were cowards. There are people who really will fight with you, and then there are others who just like to scare people. They're chicken, you know.

I never fired a gun within the city limits. I don't think I ever fired a gun in the state of Alabama. But I had one or two—or three—all the time I was there. I'm appalled by what's happened with guns in this nation in recent years; it's enough to make you cry, all the horror that's come down, but I had a .38 with a one-inch barrel in my right hip pocket for a lot of my time there.

It did save my life one time—or if it didn't save my life, it saved me from getting the tar beat out of me. I was in the Ensley neighborhood, and I came out of a building up there. I'd always get in there later than anybody else—being a nighthawk, staying up all night, and sleeping late. I'd been working, and there was one light outside in that parking lot. I had my little Volkswagen bug over on the other side, so I'm walking across that semi-dark parking lot. Suddenly, I could see that there were at least three people—maybe more—standing around my bug.

It's one of those things that'll make your heart come up in your throat. I stopped, and I heard one of them say, sotto voce, "That's him." And so I just stood there. Do you know what is the loudest quiet noise on earth? It's somebody cocking a .38. I don't remember pulling it out of my pocket but, when I cocked it, I heard the same voice say, "He's got a gun," and they melted away from the Volkswagen.

I stood there and didn't move, because I'm sure they had guns too. If I went over there and opened the door, the light was going to come on and make a nice silhouette of me, and I might be the one asking St. Peter for the old gown. So, after a while, I didn't hear anything and finally ran over there, jumped in, and started it as fast as I could. I came out of Ensley, and I don't think I got a full breath until I got into Five Points West. You ever try to drive a Volkswagen with a cocked pistol in your right hand, changing gears? Stupid!

## JOAN BAEZ AND THE RIDEY HORSE

I remember when Joan Baez came to Birmingham in 1963, at the height of her first popularity. She was playing at Miles College [a historically black college, six miles west of the city]. The demonstrations were going on downtown, and I intended to go there and see if I could make a little money, and maybe do a little good. But it tore at me where to go. I liked her songs and I liked her social action. I knew all the Carter Family stuff she was singing; it was all from where I'm from.

So I went out to the concert. She'd come down in a Volkswagen like mine, only they'd lowered it down, and it had a Hollywood muffler and some nice bumper stickers. She came out on the stage with that little midsize Martin guitar—beautiful little guitar—and she sang "We Shall Overcome." It was issued on an album, which she said was recorded in Birmingham at the height of the demonstration arrests. And it was, but there was not a black person in that audience. They were all Birmingham Southern students; the concert was at Miles, and they'd gone over there while the Miles students were downtown.

I grew up in the mountains, where the Hickses and the Harmons and the Wards all told "Jack Tales," and that concert reminded me of the one where Jack is working for the king. This big lion is causing difficulty—eating people and doing things like that—and Jack volunteers to catch it. He goes sauntering off down through there, and the lion gets after him. Jack runs and climbs up a big oak tree. He's sitting up in the tree, and the lion can't get up there. The lion starts chewing on the trunk of the tree—he's going to fell the tree with Jack in it.

He has a nice pile of sawdust there, but he doesn't have the tree down. The tree's swaying, and Jack's scared. The lion gets tired and takes a little nap. Jack's creeping down and he makes a misstep, falls, and lands right a-straddle of that lion. The lion jumps up, takes off scared, and is running through town. Some of the citizens shoot at the lion and kill it, and Jack jumps off and says, "Now what in the hell did you do that for? I was training that lion to be a ridey horse for the king."

I always thought that Joan Baez (or her agent) bragging about being in Birmingham at the height of the demonstrations was a "ridey horse" story. Anyway, she was there. Peter, Paul and Mary were there at Civic Auditorium. There were a lot of people who claimed to have been in Birmingham that I didn't particularly see there, or at least they didn't make a huge impression. I'm not sure that *I* did.

## LEAVING BIRMINGHAM

I made a little difference. But it was a big-ass job. People living in Alabama had seen what happened in Montgomery in '54 and '55. How could they keep making the same mistake? I don't think I realized it at the time, but—looking back on it—what a dumb bunch of idiots! How did anybody there think they could deal with the black community, once it was organized? It was a good reason to handle things very differently. There's an odd thing about people; they'll keep on doing what worked for them at one point, and that was what happened in Birmingham.

There used to be this sign, as you cross the Tennessee River and come into Birmingham, of how many Baptists there are in Alabama.

And these really were good people. All of them wanted to do what was right, but their question was always, "Is it nice?" My friend Ed Harris was the epitome of Birmingham, in a way. He came from a nice family. He grew up in a nice way. He went to Birmingham Southern, which was a nice place to go, and it was better for your reputation to be from Birmingham Southern than to be from the University of Alabama.

People in that state have always been sports nuts, and they still are. Compared to any other place, they're crazier than hell about it. You can't live there and not be aware of Alabama football. Is there another place on earth where people give that much of a toot about how their university is doing? No, there isn't. I live south of the University of Virginia [2013]. I don't have the foggiest notion of how Virginia is doing in anything. I know some professors up there. I know a couple of students. I go up there and talk every now and then, but I don't talk to them about what happened to me in Birmingham. They don't know anything about my involvement in any of that. I'm not sure it would interest them if they did.

I left Birmingham in early '66. Some things happened there later—there were some adjustments—but the seismic plates had shifted. It was clear how it was going to go, and there wasn't anything serious for a semi-voyeur like me to do. I'd taken some pictures. I'd written some stories. I'd been in that Sunday evening discussion group where I tried, as best I could, to get people to come over there who could talk about what was going on in Birmingham.

One of the guys in that group was Larry Fiquette. After working at the *Birmingham Post-Herald,* Larry went to the *St. Louis Post-Dispatch* and then to *The New York Times*. When I went to New York, he was there and we reestablished our little corner of Birmingham on the Upper West Side. He was a great journalist, and one thing he taught me was to always have two sources—and three is better.

There wasn't a good bluegrass band in town when I lived in Birmingham. There was one sort of a Cajun band there—believe it or not—Eddie Burns, "Country Boy" Eddie. Bluegrass comes from the Upland South. You had to go up in the Sand Mountain area of North Alabama before you started hitting music like that; it's where Rose Maddox came from originally, and the Louvins, Delmores, and Striplings.

I had a good time in Alabama, but I damn near starved to death. There wasn't enough money down there to buy a good funeral shroud!

[Carolyn Fuller's family was involved in civil rights activities in Birmingham, where she met Joe Wilson. In e-mails to the editor (in October and December of 2015), Ms. Fuller wrote:]

> Joe was a special man, who taught me at an early age about creative and resourceful ways to combat violent people. In his interviews, Joe didn't tell all the stories I heard about him when I was a young teen. I don't know why he didn't share them, but they certainly inspired me during those formative years. His actions might not have been completely legal, but they were non-violent, creative, whimsical, and effective.
>
> There are some in Birmingham who were convinced that Joe was singlehandedly responsible for the demise of the National States Rights Party, which was one very hateful, violent, racist, and anti-Semitic organization. He hung out with the NSRP, going to all their meetings. When asked why he didn't join the party, he drawled in that soft, tough-guy Appalachian accent of his that they weren't extremist enough for his tastes. (His actual words would have been much more expressive, so I won't attempt to reinvent them.)
>
> Every time he got a chance, he'd pick up matchbooks with inside covers offering all sorts of free stuff if you just mailed it in with your return address. He picked up thousands of these and would fill them out with the NSRP's office address, inundating their office with junk. He poured concrete into all their plumbing pipes. He had a live buffalo shipped to their office C.O.D. He forged an NSRP check for a substantial gift amount to B'nai B'rith.
>
> And finally, he blackmailed someone—probably Jesse Stoner—with the threat that he had enough information on him to have him arrested for what I thought was the bombing of the 16th Street Baptist Church. In return for his silence, the NSRP person had to print all the campaign literature free of charge for a local black politician running for citywide office. I am probably muddling the specifics of these stories, but you get the drift. These were not particularly safe things to be doing, but safety wasn't high on Joe's list of goals.

# New York (1966–1976)

I went from Birmingham to working for Ketchum, Inc., a Pittsburgh outfit, though I never was in Pittsburgh; I was going all over the country. Some people who worked for the organization passed through Alabama when I was there. They saw my work as a writer and said, "If you ever grow weary of this, come call us; we'll have a job for you." And they did. I did public relations/fund-raising kinds of things, some advertising—it was one of those little mini-conglomerates, you know. At one point, we had an export/import business too. Sound weird? But then a couple of years later, I was weary of them, so I went to the Oram Group on Madison Avenue in New York and stayed seven years.

I worked on civil rights fundraising there. Sometimes Supreme Court Justice Thurgood Marshall would stop by the office late in the day, when he was tired of running around the city. I'd go in, and the receptionist would say, "Shhh, Thurgood's asleep in there."

## ARCHIE GREEN AND FOLKLORE

Our company had an office in Atlanta, and that office fell under my supervision. Somehow, in Atlanta, I heard about legislation that was under consideration to start the American Folklife Center at the Library of

Congress. I called Archie Green, the folklorist, and told him I would try to help with the politicking of the thing. There had been a time, years before, when I worked for a brief period in an election of a Tennessee senator, so I kind of knew the political side of things.

I became a member of Archie's little committee. I signed up some Southern senators as sponsors for that legislation and talked to them. Those included Howard Baker and Herman Talmadge. Talmadge became an enthusiastic sponsor of the bill, only because I knew he'd grown up under the feet of Fiddlin' John Carson, who'd worked for his father [see "The Talmadge Visit"].

In New York, I enrolled in general studies at Columbia. I had an ungodly number of credit hours, in all kinds of things, stretched over five or six institutions, and no degrees in anything. I had been reading about folklore for years, and became more focused on that as an academic discipline. Archie Green thought I should go on in school, but I had two kids and a big mortgage, and no proper background to go to anyone's graduate school. So I decided not to do that. I was working at a good job, and I realized that I had entered into a part of life where you were measured more by what you could do than the degree.

I can't recall a folklorist that I ever disliked. I like all of the things that folklorists have turned up; I think they belong to me as much as they do to them. I don't tend to call myself a folklorist; I think it's OK to be an amateur. People who turn up their nose at amateurs are showing their own insecurities. To say that this body of learning is good only for teaching at universities is rather silly. That draws the circle so tight and so small it can't endure that way. This is a great body of knowledge to launch people into all kinds of fields. I wish that it would be seen that way.

## SIDE PROJECTS IN THE TRADITIONAL ARTS

I was always interested in what I'm still interested in and always pursued those things, although my income has come from a lot of different sources. When I was in New York, working on Madison Avenue, I was organizing events and making records as a hobby. I had some good microphones and a Revox HS77 prototype recorder; it was a heavy beast, nearly 100 pounds. I remember carrying it across a swinging bridge in eastern

Kentucky in the middle of the winter to record Virgil Anderson—a great old Kentucky banjo player—and there was ice on the bridge.

All of those years, I was making recordings—getting them issued on small specialty labels. Some of those things are still around. There was a little cadre of people—the Rounders among them, three kids with a Volkswagen bus—who came at it like I did, from a direction other than academia. When we were finding artists, Rich Nevins [who founded Shanachie Records in the Bronx in 1975] found Tommy Jarrell [probably the best-known fiddler, banjo player, and singer from the Round Peak area of North Carolina] and was raving. He'd been down looking for old records, and said he'd found Ben Jarrell's son; Ben Jarrell had recorded in the late 1920s with Da Costa Woltz's Southern Broadcasters. Nevins said, "You're not going to believe this—Tommy's a better fiddler than Ben was." And he was right.

# The NCTA Years (1976–2004)

Since most of the interviews from which this section was constructed took place during Joe Wilson's tenure as executive director at the National Council for Traditional Arts, the present tense is used—although Wilson retired in 2004.

It's only since 1976 that I've had the luxury of being paid to work in this field. I was in New York, a vice-president at Oram Group. The National Folk Festival Association [later that year renamed the National Council for the Traditional Arts] called me on a Sunday afternoon and said, "Would you like to come down to Washington and talk to us about a job?" I was kind of amazed, but interested. So I came and took the job and that's that. Took a heck of a pay cut, but I've never had a moment of regret. I've loved all of this, and feel I'm the luckiest guy in the world.

## NATIONAL COUNCIL FOR THE TRADITIONAL ARTS

NCTA started in 1933 in St. Louis. Sarah Gertrude Knott came from Kentucky and was a recreation worker there. She went to St. Louis during the Depression years and organized a National Folk Festival. In 1938, it came to Washington—Eleanor Roosevelt was the honorary chairman. Miss Knott was with the festival until about 1970. When she went away, they thought the festival needed someone "a little more professional," so they hired a fellow from Columbia Artists Management. The poor guy

[Leo Bernache] was miscast, and he was there for five years. [see "Beginnings of the National Folk Festival." For a more extended history of NCTA/NFFA, see *Folklife Center News* (American Folklife Center, Library of Congress) Volume XXIV, Numbers 1 and 2 (Winter and Spring 2002).]

The board included Charles Perdue, a folklorist, and Dick Spottswood, who loves the old recordings and is one of the great scholars of the whole business. Charles and Dick had met me and they called me. I never applied for the executive director's job, and didn't even know it existed. Andy Wallace was working for the Park Service then and helping NCTA [In a 2015 e-mail, Andy Wallace, associate director of NCTA from 1988–1997, wrote: "I was detailed as program director, chaired the board's program committee, and was director of the National Folk Festival from 1971 to 1975. Joe hired me in 1976 to come back and direct the festival that year, after he was hired as executive director."] When I came, the work of the organization was still primarily the National Folk Festival.

Since the beginning, the Festival has always included a potpourri of things. The NCTA always featured the Tommy Jarrells, the Kyle Creeds, the Stanley Brothers, and Bill Monroes, but it sometimes also presented the pop interpreter kinds of things, the city fad imitators. I decided that we ought to concentrate just on the basic stuff, because the other people had a lot of other places to perform. Since we can usually sell a lot of tickets, I don't book big-name bands at the National Folk Festival. I book the bands that I think deserve a hearing, that are good and deserve a little recognition. I am always amused by people who think we are running a kind of preservation hall, or assume we don't like revival musicians [see "Confessions of a Folklorist"].

I've been supported by my board. The NCTA is a collection of people—its board of directors and friends of the organization—who are interested in presenting elements of American folk culture that are varied and good. We sit somewhere between our friends in academia and our friends in show business. We respect both of them, but don't do exactly the same work that they do; we have our own work.

## EVOLUTION OF THE NATIONAL FOLK FESTIVAL

It was comfortable being at Wolf Trap Farm Park—outside of Washington, D.C.—where we held the festival from 1971 until 1982. We weren't losing money or anything. It was one of those tender traps, but a trap nonetheless, because I think the worst thing you can do with your life is to be insignificant. It seemed to me that there were other things that we ought to be doing. The Smithsonian had a wonderful Folklife Festival on the Mall, and I didn't see the need for more hors d'oeuvres to be laid on there. Since we had this Park Service tie, in 1983 we went to Cuyahoga National Recreation Area near Akron, Ohio. We did three festivals out there, and they were successful.

Then we went to Lowell, Massachusetts, and those festivals were a roaring success. I like going into places like Lowell, with these ethnic populations who came there to get an entry-level job and a foot on the rung of the upward mobility ladder. It's also the place where the mills closed down first and you had the first Rust Belt. It was a town with a tough reputation; people didn't come to Lowell, but we got more than 100,000 people to show up in the middle of that town. It astonished Lowell the first time. They came from Cambridge, they came from Portland, they came from Boston. People from Lowell didn't come the first year; they didn't come the second year either—they thought it was a fluke. But by the third year, they were there.

Getting people to come there really proved something. When we were ready to leave for the next city location, the Lowellians brought me up for a meeting and said, "Well, we know that you think we ought to do a regional festival here. How about you help us with these things which we need help with. You can take the National Folk Festival name and buzz off with it. We'd like to change the name to Lowell Folk Festival and increase the attendance next year by fifteen percent." Well, we did that and it's still percolating along—it's the second largest free folk festival in the United States.

Working in places like that, I think that's a part of our job—urban revitalization. I think that we need to make allies with people who want to preserve central parts of cities. Paul Tsongas [then U.S. Senator from Massachusetts] walked up to me at the third festival and said, "This is a wonderful thing. What can I do for you?"

They've since [in 2000] put in a summer music series. They've built a new arena. It's suddenly a town with an entertainment theme. It's bringing lots of people in. It's got a new minor league baseball team and a new stadium downtown. I think anyone from there will tell you that the roaring success of the Folk Festival helped trigger that kind of thinking about the town. It made the other things seem less risky.

If you are trying to put a big crowd together, there are some things you really need to learn. It's important to build partnerships of trust with people who have strength in areas where you need strength. If you can have a little team of people sitting around the table—the chief electrician for the city, the chief of police, the fire chief, the Department of Sanitation, and the mayor—then you've got some really strong partners. It's nice to have the television stations as a partner with you too.

Before the Soviet Union collapsed, we did a tour of music from the USSR [*Voices of the Soviet Union*, 1990]. We had a KGB guy come along to check us out in advance—he was supposed to be a cultural guy, but he was a KGB officer. I took him up to Lowell, and he looked around and went to a meeting there. After it was over, he said to me, "Who's in charge there? Was the mayor in charge?" and I said, "No," and he says, "The Park Superintendent?" "No." "You, you're in charge!" and I said, "No, no. We sit around the table." He says, "You sit around this table and talk? And what do you do if someone doesn't do what they're supposed to do?" And I said, "Well, they wouldn't be able to sit at the table anymore." And he said, "Democracy [is] very complicated."

One of the suppositions folklorists have is that there are all kinds of wonderful local culture that local citizens don't know a thing about. That's usually true in part. There are always lots of local things that none of us knows anything about. But that's not enough. In the festival we did in East Lansing, Michigan [1999–2001], people loved seeing [national acts] Eileen Ivers and Natalie MacMaster up there playing the fiddle. But Les Ross, a great harmonica player who came from the Upper Peninsula of Michigan with a town hall band, they loved him too.

It's always nice to know that some of the people from within the state—some of the locals—are as good as those we bring in. People don't like to have you rub their nose in learning. The less you jawbone them, and the more you let them figure out for themselves, the better the lesson. That kind of thinking and that kind of learning endures, and changes people—changes their thinking.

We've continued to do festivals, of course, and help other people organize them, but we've moved a bit beyond that because we think there are other ways to present. We probably put more effort into tours now than we do into festivals.

## NCTA TOURS IN THE U.S.

I believe there are forty-eight states which have had tours. For a small organization, that's rather extensive. And we will continue to do touring, because you can take material back to the places of its origin that way. Being from the Blue Ridge, I am particularly aware of the fact that it's not easy to hear the best of Appalachian music there. It's easy enough in Washington, D.C., Baltimore, Cleveland—most any large city. But if you are in Mountain City, Tennessee, near where I'm from, the good bands don't come all that often.

So we've tried to do folk arts touring. It's difficult, because communities don't always have the kind of presenting organizations that you need. At the same time, we've avoided doing what is done with most touring, which is to take it to college campuses. We have a phrase about that—"we try not to stimulate the overstimulated." Most of the people we deal with have never sponsored a concert of any kind before. They decide to try it and we tell them how to do it; it's pioneering work. It's a grassroots organizing kind of thing.

The size of the community sometimes is not a good predictor of what can happen there. *The Cowboy Tour* [1983–1984, see "The Cowboy Tour" in *Roots Music in America*], for example, went to Medora, North Dakota. It's a cattle town with a population of 80-some full-time residents. There are more people there in the summer because it's near Teddy Roosevelt's ranch—which is a national park, so there are park visitors and some businesses that cater to park visitors–but it's still a tiny place. We had over 600 people there and filled the hall. We had a wonderful time in Medora, and thought it was one of the finest places we ever performed. I think it's better to have 600 in Medora than 6,000 in one of our major urban areas, because those are 600 people who don't get to see the best of their culture all that often.

I roomed for a whole tour once with Howard Armstrong, the black violinist from LaFollette, Tennessee. He was Appalachian like me, but he also played some jazz and blues, and he would wake up early in the morning. I had a Martin guitar with me that I was carrying as an extra, in case someone broke a string onstage. I'd have that beast in tune, so I could walk right up there on stage and stick it on them, so we could keep the show going. Howard would wake up every morning very early—a couple of hours before I was up—and he'd sneak over and get the guitar, then he'd sit there and finger-pick. I'd have these two-hour concerts of stunning blues and jazz. There are lots of records of him on the violin—with Martin, Bogan, and Armstrong; the Four Keys; and the other people he recorded with—but that solo guitar never got recorded, as far as I know, and I'm sorry about that.

Some of our touring things have been ahead of their time. In 1982, we first toured *Raices Musicales*—regional music from Mexico. There are Mexicans all over this country. We had a great marimba, a Tex-Mex band, mariachis, a Veracruz band, and some guys from northern New Mexico. We played three tours of that—from New England to the West Coast and as far south as Kentucky—in lots of places, but the concept was a little early. Some of our state folk-arts people weren't ready for it at that point.

## TOURING THE WORLD

We helped the United States Information Agency people put together tours to other nations. Some of the overseas touring has been very interesting.

On one of those tours, I was in Papua New Guinea with an American Indian troupe. Papua New Guinea is full of literally stone-age people who only met Western civilization—or any kind of civilization other than their own—in the 1930s. There are 800 languages there—not dialects, but fully formed languages. About 30,000 to 40,000 of these remote people come together for singing and dancing in what they call the Sing-Sing at Port Moresby. Those people know very little about North America, but they do know that there are indigenous people here, and they think our indigenous people are like them.

The diplomatic officials with us were saying, "They might not listen to you at all." Well, they sure misjudged those people, because they listened very raptly. The Zunis—led by Fernando Cellicion—started the "Sunrise Song," which is a nice harmony song that the elders sing from the top of the pueblo in the ancient Zuni language. Everything was quite still. Then the Lakota hoop dancer comes bounding across the stage. He has a single hoop—rather small—and he's twirling, and he bounces back and forth a couple of times, and then he leaps through the hoop. It is an amazing feat of physical prowess. There's a tape of that somewhere, and you can hear 30,000 people gasp. It was as good a 25-minute show as has ever been done, and it was well accepted.

I remember being in Sri Lanka one time with The Whites. Ricky Skaggs, now a country music superstar, was playing violin. Jerry Douglas, the great Dobro guitarist, was also with them. We were going to play in an ambassador's backyard, but one of those torrential rains came up, so we moved into the living room. We packed 200 or so people in there and did it all acoustic. That ambassador kept in touch with me for years; it went over so well that he thought I was some kind of special genius. He didn't realize it was just his having a good living room and the moment. Artists feed on audiences and audiences on artists, and if you can get a great intimacy working, it's a good thing [see "Rediscovering Cambodia's Royal Ballet"].

## NEW PROJECTS

Life continues to be exciting, with new projects going on. Beyond tours, we've done some videotapes, and we've been doing some film, and we've issued some recordings, radio programs—we've tried to work as broadly as we can. [Joe narrated approximately fifty radio programs produced by WDUQ-FM, Pittsburgh, and distributed nationally throughout the public radio system. Fragments are periodically streamed on the NCTA website.]

I'm talking [in 2000] with the Park Service about managing the Blue Ridge Music Center, to be built on the Blue Ridge Parkway, near the North Carolina-Virginia state line. [The Blue Ridge Music Center opened in 2002 and is operated by the National Park Service, through a partnership with the Blue Ridge Parkway Foundation.] I've dealt with it from the congressional level on down. We have the money to build part of it, but there has to be some more money raised. And the Park Service, as part of the legislation, has no money to run the thing; Congress is putting zero into that. So, whoever runs it—us or anyone else—has to go raise that money, and they have to earn whatever they can at the center. That is the way you work with the parks. Bring them ideas that mesh with their ideas and you'll find great partners. Come with your hand out, and they'll think you're a dork—and you will be.

We worked on a new park in Nicodemus, a little black town on the high plains of western Kansas. It was settled by freed slaves from Kentucky who rode the train as far west as they could, then walked across the prairie and started the town, first living in dugouts and then in sod houses. It got up to where it had 800 or 900 people. Now it's dwindled back down to 51, but there are still people who lived there who come back every year. So, they made it into a historical site [in 1996] and got NCTA to come out and help put together a program for it.

We also worked on Cane River, another new park, south of Baton Rouge, Louisiana. Cane River Creole Park [opened in 1994] is a plantation where there is a history of slavery. It's also the area where there were Creoles of color, black folk who owned slaves, some in considerable numbers—the Creole aristocracy. If those people can deal with the complicated reality of that time, then why can't the rest of us?

We have a variety of things going on with the Park Service. We are producing a compact disc recording for distribution by the New Orleans Jazz National Historical Park. It deals with the history of jazz, the folk origins of jazz, and features some of the old vintage recordings. We are choosing the recordings, and, literally, making and packaging the things that will be sold from there.

We're working on all kinds of other things we think are interesting. It's still exciting to get up in the morning and come to work. We can get to our customers in ways that we were never able to before, and it demands that we be better. Any little kid who wants to can find us now. We're selling tickets online. We can take your credit card, and it's secure. The ticket will be in the mail to you by the next morning, and we'll have your money in our bank. We're still learning all of this—we have a couple of staff members who are good at this kind of thing.

All of the people who've worked here, they're my peers and always will be. But the people—the great artists, the people who come from the country church—I love that we are able to give voice to music, speech, craft, and so forth—great voices that need to be heard in this country. I guess this reveals me as a folk romantic. I believe that putting people together around their music and their dance and their foodways—particularly the common ordinary working folks—has a way of lessening prejudice and promotes things that need very much to be promoted.

# Back to the New River (2004–2015)

Plagued by health difficulties, Joe Wilson stepped away from management of the National Council for the Traditional Arts in 2004, but remained active with the organization until his death in May of 2015. Two projects in Southwest Virginia held Joe's particular focus.

He and Blue Ridge Parkway Superintendent Gary Everhart had conceived the Blue Ridge Music Center in 1987. Joe worked doggedly on its funding and development for 24 years. The City of Galax, Virginia, donated much of the 2,500-acre mountaintop site. Ground was broken in 2000, the Center opened in 2002, and permanent exhibits based on Joe's vision and writings were installed in 2011.

Joe and Todd Christensen—then Associate Director for the Virginia Department of Housing and Community Development—met in 2002 at a creative economy conference in Asheville, North Carolina, and envisioned The Crooked Road: Virginia's Heritage Music Trail. The 333-mile route now connects nine major venues, more than sixty affiliated venues and festivals, nineteen counties, four cities, and more than fifty towns and communities on scenic byways in the Blue Ridge and coalfields regions of Virginia. In 2006, Joe authored *A Guide to the Crooked Road* and narrated its two bound-in music CDs.

Upon retirement, Joe and his wife Kathy James (they married in 1988) moved to Fries, Virginia, a historic mill town on both the Crooked Road and the New River—completing a circle, as Joe was born along that same river some sixty miles upstream (Joe was fond of telling audiences that the New River, like the Nile, flows from south to north). Joe considered Fries to be one of the true birthplaces of country music [see "Fries: Where the Music Began" in *Roots Music in America*]. There—between musical, lobbying, and consulting trips—he threw himself even more deeply into lifelong avocations of reading and writing, mostly on topics of history and folk arts.

You track through this life, you can have an effect, and you can be beneficial in lots of ways. I never had a graduate school experience. I barely had an undergraduate school experience. I love and admire folklorists, and consider myself their peer, but I'm also a hillbilly, and some of my other peers are back where I come from. It makes me look at "the folk" maybe a little differently.

## COLLABORATION AND ADVOCACY

If I've learned anything that might be of value to others, it's that you need to put together groups of people to do things. You can do so much more with a group of organizations than you can with a single organization. In a city, for example, it's better if the state can work with the city fathers, and the city with the state, and the city with private entities.

I've always thought it's important to stay involved with politics—or democracy, or whatever it is. To get anything done, you have to have access to some resources and—in a lot of cases—those are controlled by elected representatives. So I've never minded taking my case to them, and, if anyone was stepping on some part of my anatomy, I went over and tried to find the foot removal team.

Maybe I learned some of this from Archie Green. Archie had a commitment to the academy, a commitment to working folk and to occupations that I admired. He had the courage to take on things politically. I'll never quit taking on things political.

People tend to be incredibly naive about how things get done. They think all you have to do is hire some lobbyist who lives on a diet of olive oil and other slippery stuff. They don't realize that members of Congress like to hear from people back home. It's not enough to "send in cards and letters," because the people who want to do away with all government involvement in culture can produce more letters in a day than we can produce in the rest of our time on earth. You have to sit down and talk to elected officials—invest a little time into it.

Years ago, I went to meet Rick Boucher [former U.S. Representative from Southwest Virginia] about the Blue Ridge Music Center. As I started talking about it, and as we got further into it, Rick started sliding forward until he was sitting on the last inch of his chair. When we left that room, he was more enthusiastic than I was. I hadn't taken him through Folklore 101 or anything else; I just told him what this was all about, and he bought in. It's in his district, it's his people, and he knows his people.

It's best not to be cynical about politicians. God knows there are plenty of people in Congress that I am cynical about—but they gave me a reason to feel that way. A lot of people in this country think all politicians are the same. That's not true; public service is a really important calling. If you fall into that kind of cynicism about government, then you've done a bad thing.

People who serve in an elected office understand, almost instinctively, that part of their constituency is very interested in what folk arts people do. But you have to go sit down with them and talk to them about it. You tell them the truth. You tell them why this is important, why this is good, and you tell them this is some of the treasure of the country—material that has to be dealt with—and you tell them you don't have enough money.

## THE VALUE OF VERNACULAR ARTS

Organizations like NCTA can show that art is widespread among the American people, and woven into the fabric of our lives. We can show that there are aesthetic standards and high quality everywhere. In this country, that hasn't always been accepted and is still a controversial thing. We borrow too many of our arts from Western European elite systems. We put those arts on a pedestal while ignoring the home-grown things of quality that exist all around us. We can help everyday people to understand that art isn't something someone else has, that they send out to you occasionally.

One of the problems for any organization that presents performance is that there's a belief in this country—that goes back to its very founding over two centuries ago—that performances are insubstantial. But what has been learned over the years through studies in psychology and anthropology is that performance isn't at all insubstantial. Good performance can be enlightening, deeply educational, and have enduring effect.

Music is an ability to hear, among other things. It is an ability to tell when something's in tune and when it's out of tune. You reach for the note and you miss it or you hit it. The timing works or it doesn't. And for some reason, I had a gift with that. I can tell when something's working.

Most people don't choose their music by what they hear. They choose it by social context, by what their generation is listening to. I don't think I ever chose music that way. (Well, perhaps I became engrossed with folk music because I grew up in that—so that is socialization in a way.) I live in the Blue Ridge Mountains. Rain falls here and runs out of my yard into the New River, flows into the Ohio River, and ends up in the Mississippi River. I quickly learned that there were other people who had musics that grew from the same kinds of roots.

The ephemera that goes by so fast is the top ten—the flash of the moment–because it has a date stuck to it. It is a leaf from the tree; it doesn't add a ring of growth to it. It has its function. I don't put it down, but it doesn't endure. It gets ground up and goes into mulch; it doesn't completely disappear, but it doesn't exist again in that form.

God knows there are a lot of tone-deaf people walking around, heaven help them. That's much worse than colorblindness, and nearly as bad as total blindness. I figure that anybody who can listen to Muzak or a top-40 station all day—and like it—has a very bad problem.

One of the curses of the pop culture market is that it makes faddists out of people. They are not sure of their taste, and they move from this, to this, to this, to this. If I had any kind of contribution I could make to this field, it would be to get people who worry about their taste to realize that their taste is just as damn good as anybody else's. It's OK if they like bluegrass, or old-time, or any other form of music. Whatever you like is really whatever you like.

## CHANGE AND OPPORTUNITY

We have the ability now to put lots of things online. Some kid in my little home place of Trade, Tennessee, on the western slope of the Blue Ridge may want to find out about Tom Ashley or Gilliam Banmon Grayson. There is this great set of recordings of Tom Ashley, Doc Watson, Clint Howard, and Fred Price on the Folkways label. Do you know, there has never been one of those sold in that county? There is no record store there.

In the 1970s, I recorded Clint Howard and Fred Price for Rounder, and I got their hometown newspaper in Mountain City to sell that recording. Almost one out of ten people—more than 800 in a county of 10,000 people—bought it, and that's astounding! It's not that the market's not there, it's that the mechanism doesn't reach there. Record labels are bordering on becoming obsolete. Online, we can reach almost everywhere.

I've never joined the "rescue the perishing" school of folklore. Go back to the early recordings—in the twenties and the thirties—of something like, say, Sacred Harp music. The people recognized that they were dealing with an old form and were certain that it was going to disappear. The singers were all middle-aged or older people, so they hurried themselves to record this, to get it down. Well it's still roaring along, and all of the singers are still middle-aged and older. I don't know whether you have to hear the hoofbeats of destiny or what the hell it is, but it's a music for the older citizens.

I think that everything changes, and is always in a state of flux. If you ever succeed at stopping anything dead in its tracks, you will have killed the hell out of it. Preservation is not one of my goals. I even think that there are a lot of things that ought to die out—and, for some of them, the sooner the better. I wouldn't care if all the canned music machines blew up, and if there was a big sucking sound, and all the video games and television sets went away. I'd hardly miss them at all.

With all of the media that we have, the thing that really matters is for people to hear each other and to meet each other face-to-face. Encountering someone from a few feet away has an impact, a force, and a power that's never matched by anything else. Some of the best work we can do in making the world a little easier to live in is to let people really see each other. It takes down barriers. It may sound simplistic, but in the long run that matters more than any other kind of diplomacy.

There are forces in the country that worry me. I worry about how few people vote in this country. I think democracy is a terribly important form of government, and that we need to preserve and extend it. I worry that money and fame will become the criteria for election to public office, which could get our country into a bad situation.

This country has not yet come to grips with the history of slavery. One of the great founding principles of this country was slavery. A lot of the country was built on the sweat of black people. And with all the museums to all of these things, there's no great museum to slavery. [The Whitney Plantation, a museum devoted to slavery in the U.S., opened in 2014 in Wallace, Louisiana.] The country still has to deal with recognizing and dealing with it factually—what happened, what it was about, and what its effects were.

I don't think anybody can be free until everybody is free. In my lifetime we've seen a major shift toward equality. Anyone who tells you that nothing has changed is full of prune juice. It has changed, and it has changed a hell of a lot, but coming to grips with our history—that little turn in the mind that we need to deal with it—hasn't happened yet. I'd like to see that happen.

I always think that the future will probably be better at planning itself than I am. The wish to control the future is the ultimate conceit. The search for security is one of the things that keeps people from growing—keeps them hunkered down in jobs they should have quit. It's awfully hard to starve to death in this society. I have a little bit of an edge here; if you come from a two-room house, everything looks easy. But even if you come from a house with three bathrooms, it's easy to be fearful of the future and too conservative in your approach to life.

I want people to know how to learn, because the process we're going through is one of learning all the time. As for what you should know: being able to write well, being able to research and think logically—those are terribly important. The old liberal arts education—a broad education—is more important now than ever in these times of great specialization. I think theory is a great way to understand things. It's good to have filters and separation media of all kinds, so we can see how things behave apart from the rest of life. But you have to keep in mind that the separation itself is artificial. We are a part of that larger cosmos.

It's what you do with your knowledge that's critical. The best of institutions are guided by singular visions. If you don't have a spark plug—someone who really, really, cares and is passionate about it—things die.

It's true of almost everything, and in the arts it's especially true. I don't want to be respectable; I just want to get things done.

## FINALE

I come from a family of musicians, but I'm not patient enough to practice music. I am a little hard on myself if my fingers don't do what my ears say they should. I have a guitar at home, and I sometimes get it out from under the bed in the morning and play some chords and sing. My little dog, Jake, sits there and listens and sits on his butt and looks at me, and then he'll walk over and sit by the door and say, "I've listened to that stuff. You should give me a walk."

I'm having a good time [2005]. I'll keep on doing what I've done, still find things that I'm passionate about and that seem important to deal with. I am writing a little more now, and I've got maybe a couple of books that might get churned out in the next three or four years—if I've got three or four years. I'm running on borrowed parts. I had a kidney transplant back in 2001, and I had some serious health matters there for a while, but I've had the benefit of some very good medical help.

If you peer down into the abyss, and see the dude down there shoveling coal, it does give you pause. You focus a little more on what's important to you, you know. And you yell down and say: "Buford, you can go to hell. I'm not coming. I'm going to work awhile."

I've made most of the mistakes that anyone can make, and some of them twice. I'm not blessed with getting it the first time; sometimes I have to be hit with a big hammer. I always tried to be where things were interesting. I figure you've got a little trip here. You're born, and you travel along, and suddenly you're gone, and that's your one shot at being worth more than a rabbit. And a rabbit never does any serious harm, but he doesn't do much serious good either. Well I shouldn't say he doesn't do any harm—if he's in Australia, he's a damn nuisance.

### SOURCES

Anderson, Laura. Interview With Joe Wilson (14 October 2013). Birmingham Civil Rights Institute Oral History Project, Birmingham, Alabama.

Belanus, Betty. "Collaborations: An Interview with Joe Wilson." *Folklore Forum* (Indiana University) 31:2 (2000).

Ferguson, Mark Lynn. "Never Be Boring: How a Self-Educated Mountain Man Became a Living Legend." *Smoky Mountain Living* June/July 2015.

Fuller, Carolyn. "Re: Joe Wilson." Message to Fred Bartenstein. 8 October 2015. E-mail.

Fuller, Carolyn. "Re: Joe Wilson." Message to Fred Bartenstein. 22 December 2015. E-mail.

Lohman, Jon. StoryCorps Interview with Joe Wilson (24 May 2005). Washington, D.C.

Rosenberg, Neil. Interview with Joe Wilson (6 June 1979). Washington, D.C.

Snyder, Eugenia. "Joe Wilson: A Bluegrasser at the Helm of the NCTA." *Bluegrass Unlimited* April 1986.

Topping, Brett. "An Interview with Joe Wilson." *Folklife Center News* (American Folklife Center, Library of Congress) January-March 1986. (The audiotape is archived at AFC 1986/042: Joe Wilson Interview for Folklife Center News Collection.)

Wilson, Joe. "Lucky Joe." Message to family members. 19 September 2012. E-mail.

# TRADE, TENNESSEE

# Introduction to Trade Articles

Napoleon's line that "history is a set of lies agreed to" has some currency. Conventional history as it's normally written depicts a surfer, and the surfer is the leader of the time. The surfer is riding on the curl of the wave, screaming all the way to the shore that he's pulling the ocean. Trade, Tennessee, is a part of the ocean. I like understanding the ocean better than I do surfers.

Trade has a complex and long history, and I'm very interested in that place; at this point it's as much an intellectual interest as it is a family one. My family's been there for 200 years, so it's hard to be disassociated from the people that are there. But it's also nice to follow a place over time, and understand how all of the events that swirled around over the world affected this little place. And to look at what was happening there and try to imagine or find out why.

Trade is a very, very small place—253, I think. It's always been small, and it probably won't ever get any bigger. But there have been important

---

From "An Interview with Joe Wilson," *Folklife Center News*, American Folklife Center, Library of Congress, January-March 1986.

things happen there. We've had bank robbers and counterfeiters and preachers and paperhangers, a whole panoply.

Once, years ago, I was sitting on the store porch there and a tourist drove up from Florida—Florida plate on his car. He was traveling around the South taking pictures of Confederate memorials and antebellum houses. And, of course, the mountains were Union, so he hadn't been able to find any Confederate memorials there; there aren't any, you know. And so he asked about the memorials and somebody said, "Don't have any of them." So he says, "What about historic homes, do you have any historic homes?" "Don't think so." And he says, "Any big men born around here?" And the answer was, "Nah, best we can do is babies."

# Trading at Trade

The easternmost and oldest community in the state of Tennessee is located south of Mountain City, near the border with North Carolina. Trade is named for an ancient Indian trading ground that was used in colonial times, before the area was settled by permanent residents.

Called "the Trading Ground" and "the Trade Place" by packhorse traders engaged in fur trading with Indians, Trade is located five miles northwest of another historic Blue Ridge place: "the Meat Camp." Meat Camp is located on the North Carolina side of the state line, on the opposite side of Snake Mountain. It was named by hunters from the Piedmont and Yadkin Valley in North Carolina, who hunted, salted, and kept game meat in log structures until they accumulated packhorse train loads. The Trading Ground is by far the older of these two historic sites.

Both Trade and Meat Camp are located on the over-mountain Indian trail. This ancient trace can be found on the earliest maps of the area. Before its use by Indians, this trace was a buffalo trail. Buffalo moved

---

Unpublished. Joe Wilson wrote: "This was written in 1974, when I was working in New York and my desk had an up-close view of the Chrysler building. Was it that urban morass below that made me want to write about a mountain pass? I finished it, but never submitted it to anyone. I was awfully busy then, and writing was largely a hobby used to ease pressure."

in early summer to the high-mountain balds where grass grew in profusion. In the heavily forested period before settlement—when it was said a squirrel could go from the Eastern Seaboard to the Mississippi River without touching the ground—the balds were important grasslands for grazing animals. The buffalo herds came down from the mountains in the fall, and they were good road builders.

The ancient buffalo and Indian trail follows Roan's Creek through the gorge south of Shouns and Mountain City, and continues up the main valley of the creek to the junction of Route 67 and US 421 in Trade. Roan's Creek flows southwesterly and is named for a roan horse owned by a later traveler: Daniel Boone. During one of their trips to Kentucky, Old Roan became lame, so Daniel turned her loose, hid his saddle, and walked to Kentucky. On returning, he found she had healed and grown fat, so he retrieved his saddle and rode back to the Yadkin Valley.

The Trading Ground is the relatively flat area adjacent to US 421 in front of the Trade Community Center, extending to the present junction of Route 67 and US 421. Near here, the old buffalo and Indian trail turns up the Modock Road toward the gap between Snake and Rich Mountains.

What circumstances put the Trading Ground where it is? One can hazard several guesses.

It may have been like other trading sites in paleo-America in having a history of Indian trading that preceded the arrival of Europeans. We know that some pre-European trade routes by Indians extended over hundreds of miles, and that there were numerous traditional "trade place" sites. We also know that the Trade site has many Indian artifacts; archeologists seem not to have dug in Trade, but every boy who followed a plow or harrow there was rewarded with a rich harvest of points and other stone tools.

Another guess: traders managing an early pack train may have been discouraged by the steep climb up and down the two sides of Snake Mountain. Perhaps they decided to sit down on the first big flat place on the Indian trail and start buying and selling.

One of the ancient rules of geographic history is that trade is almost always the cutting edge of exploration. It precedes hunting and the keeping of animals, as a place develops permanent residents. This is certainly true of Trade, Tennessee. No one kept an account of early happenings there, so we must rely on chance mention by travelers, cryptic official records, and other stray bits of information that fall to us.

We know that the Trading Ground was part of a far-flung fur trading empire established in the Southeast as early as the 1640s, although we don't know exactly when the Trading Ground came into use. A key staging ground for the English fur trade was Fort Henry—originally operated by Abraham Wood—in eastern Virginia, near the present city of Petersburg (named for Peter Jones, Wood's son-in-law). Packhorse trading routes extended hundreds of miles into the interior. Some workers were gone with their pack trains for many weeks, and furs rivaled tobacco as a primary cash crop of the Southern colonies.

Trading continued for generations, and in the 1750s as many as 50,000 deerskins a year were coming to Virginia from the Carolina frontier. A single deerskin was called "a buck" and became the unit of trade. The term continued after the dollar became the unit of trade and it too became "a buck."

In his book *History of the Dividing Line*, an account of a survey establishing the border between Virginia and North Carolina, William Byrd of Westover [Charles City County, Virginia] tells of crossing the trading path near the mountains on November 15, 1728. Byrd said the goods going down the trail were " . . . guns, powder, shot, hatchets (which the Indians call tomahawks), kettles, blankets, cutlery, brass rings, and trinkets." Byrd said those wares were made into packs and carried on horses, and the traders were able to travel twenty miles a day. He said, "Formerly a hundred horses have been employed in one of these Indian caravans." Byrd thought this trade vital to the future of the colonies.

Byrd's account tells of another trade item of great importance: ginseng. Byrd said of it, "This plant is of high esteem in China, and sells for its weight in silver." Ginseng was to increase in importance in the decades that followed, and fueled the American clipper ship trade with China.

Judge Samuel Cole Williams, dean of Tennessee historians, believed Trade was the first place where English was spoken in Tennessee. In his book, *Dawn of the Tennessee Valley and Tennessee History* (1937), the former Tennessee Supreme Court jurist detailed the 1673 path of James Needham and Gabriel Arthur from Abraham Wood's Fort Henry along "a well-worn Indian trail" to Trade and beyond.

The Virginia trader-owners who sent out the pack trains tended to remain near coastal shipping points, and it was mainly hired hands who went down the trails. A few, such as Julius Caesar Dugger and Andrew Greer, came to what is now Johnson County, but there is no documentation of them as primary traders at Trade. The Indians who came to Trade to barter furs and ginseng may, in many cases, have traveled greater distances than the eastern Virginia traders.

One of the remarkable attributes of the region between the Tennessee River and the New River in Virginia was the absence of resident Indians. Trading, hunting, and war parties used the over-mountain trail and Great Valley Road, but there are no credible reports of villages or even individual Indian families in the area. Daniel Boone told that he was once robbed of a cache of furs near the head of Roan's Creek (which would mean at or near Trade). But it is likely that the robbers—like Boone—were traveling.

A plethora of artifacts of all kinds at Trade and elsewhere in the region is testimony to the abundant presence of Indians in earlier times. But Indians told that a series of wars between northern and southern tribes made the area an Indian's no-man's-land in the generations immediately before people of European ancestry arrived. J.G.M. Ramsey, who wrote *Annals of Tennessee to the End of the Eighteenth Century* in 1853, said the area was a common hunting ground for Shawnee, Cherokee, and others.

There are other good reasons why Trade served as a meeting place in ancient times. It may not seem so today, but it was then a crossroads. The pack trains followed the over-mountain trail up the Lewis Fork of the Yadkin toward Deep Gap. The trail wound from Deep Gap to the South Fork of the New River (the fork that flows near present-day Boone). It took the Meat Camp branch from the South Fork, across the gap between Snake and Rich Mountains, and down the northwestern slope of the Snake to the Trading Ground. North of the Trading Ground, the trail followed Roan's Creek to near Mountain City, and then entered the valley of Laurel Creek, to deliver the traveler near the relative flats of a branch of Virginia's Great Valley Road, where it meets the Tennessee Valley.

Viewed on a detailed topographic or relief map, it is a route that makes much sense. It avoids crossing steep mountain ranges: the Stone, Forge, Iron, and Holston. In an 1897 letter to the Daughters of the American Revolution, Henry Greer told why he was absolutely certain Daniel Boone used this route. Henry said he'd learned Boone's route from his grandfather, who had learned it from his father, and added, "It was then much the easiest way to go, and Mister Boone was not a fool."

Trade is also near the headwaters of the New River. If one follows Route 67 to the North Carolina state line at Trade (where it becomes North Carolina Route 88), a spring and small creek in the valley to the right show the beginning of one branch of the North Fork of the New. The branch begins at a spring above 5,000 feet on Snake Mountain, one of the highest points on the New River.

Since water flows downhill, it is the nature of rivers to begin at their highest point and flow to their lowest point. By its connections to the Ohio and the Mississippi, one may surmise that the lowest point on the New River is the Gulf of Mexico. Its beginning point is disputed. Some geographers say the New River begins at Blowing Rock, but that location is lower in altitude than the spring on Snake Mountain above Trade and the Trading Ground.

The New River is relatively rare among North American waterways in that it flows north. The New River crosses Virginia and West Virginia before joining the Ohio River. That meandering river, with its gentle grades and wide banks, was a frequent road for emigrants who moved down the New River valley from the place where it crosses the Great Valley Road of Virginia.

It has an inappropriate name. It was called "New" to distinguish it from the James and other east-flowing rivers encountered earlier by explorers and traders. It is, in fact, a remnant of the oldest river system in North America: the Teays of prehistory, one of the oldest rivers on earth—comparable in age to the Nile, and the Tigris and Euphrates of the Fertile Crescent.

So, in early times, Trade was a place with river valleys in three directions and an ancient well-worn road—albeit one that was steep and rough even for packhorses. But the primary factor that brought pack traders, Boone, and others to Trade was the Indian and buffalo path. Travelers did not have to cut their way through thickets of vines, saw briars, and saplings in order to follow that trail.

The extraordinary difficulty of mountain travel in those times is described in two famous accounts. In 1728, William Byrd did not run his line between the two royal colonies as far as the Blue Ridge, because he had too much difficulty with the foothills. In his 1752 diary, Moravian Bishop Augustus Spangenberg told of the struggles of his exploration party in crossing the Blue Ridge, a few miles north of the trail. The good bishop admired the mountains, but built his colony for believers at Salem (now Winston-Salem), in terrain that is much easier to traverse.

The first map of a portion of what is now Johnson County and Laurel Creek is the 1749 Peter Jefferson and Joshua Frye map that extended Byrd's dividing line westward. Peter Jefferson was the father of the nation's third president, Thomas Jefferson.

The first permanent settlers of European ancestry seem to have arrived while the Trading Ground was still being used. In fact, the buying of ginseng for the China trade and other herbs at Trade continued until the Civil War, long after the skins of deer, beaver, and bear stopped being the major trade items for the area. There's still a small ginseng harvest in the area, and a few Americans seem to have adopted the age-old Chinese superstition that the herb is a cure-all for sexual dysfunction; modern medical research has found no use for the herb in the pharmacopoeia, and it appears to be completely useless.

The movement of settlers into the fringe of the Watauga area began in the 1750s, and accelerated during the 1760s. Most historians writing about the area follow Ramsey. That fine Tennessee historian reveals no awareness of the fringe of settlements between the Yadkin settlements in North Carolina and the Watauga settlements in the Elizabethton-Jonesborough corridor. He wrote in 1853, a century after settlement, and seems to have interviewed persons who had little if any knowledge of the easternmost fringe of Tennessee. Though Trade is at least technically part of the Watauga settlements, none of its earliest citizens are named among the early Watauga settlers. Yet we know the names of some that were contemporaries of persons that were named.

The term "the lost provinces" was once applied to the trans-Blue Ridge counties of North Carolina, usually referring to Ashe and Watauga. The term could have more accurately been applied to neighboring Johnson County, surely more "lost" from Tennessee than Ashe and Watauga ever were from North Carolina. There is good reason for this separation. For persons residing in what is now Johnson County, the downriver route to Sycamore Shoals and other central Watauga locations was extremely difficult to traverse.

A bit of humor about such matters survives from Reuben Dotson. "Uncle Reuben" said he had lived in five states but had never moved, and was living in the house he was born in. When Uncle Reuben was born there in the 1760s, residents thought they were in colonial Virginia. They later learned they were in colonial North Carolina. Then they found themselves residents of Wayne County in the abortive state of Franklin. An act of Congress later made them resident of The Territory South of the Ohio River. Finally, in 1796, they were made part of the state of Tennessee.

Uncle Reuben always told the census takers that he was born in Virginia. At age 100, he tended three acres of corn in a new ground. His house at Trade was positioned to be safe from the Indian and trader traffic on the nearby—but somewhat dangerous—well-traveled road. To reach the site of Uncle Reuben's abode, one must continue three miles north of the Trading Ground, in the Trade Valley on Highway 421, to what is now called the Bulldog Road. Almost a mile up that road, the visitor turns left on the Eggers Road. After almost another mile, the Eggers Road comes to a dead end among high ridges. Uncle Reuben lived in a huge log house here, and his son, Allen Dotson—sheriff of Johnson County before the Civil War—lived nearby in another.

By climbing and descending a high ridge to the north, the Dotson family could be at the Trading Ground in thirty minutes. But seen from the Trading Ground, the mountains to the south must have seemed steep, forbidding, and impenetrable. Nevertheless, the houses—built of huge chestnut logs—had upstairs rifle slots.

Alfred Dotson, one of many grandsons of Uncle Reuben, was born before the Civil War and lived until after the Great Depression. Noted for his hospitality, kindness, and gentility, "Grandpa Dotson" spoke of the many generations he had seen leave this high mountain valley, some with fifteen or sixteen children in a family. "We need to pray that they don't all come back," he said. "They'd need to stand on each other's shoulders for us to accommodate them."

# Henry Main

## *Johnson County Pioneer*

Henry Harrison Main was born in Cheshire, England, and came to Maryland before the American Revolution. He was a ditcher who built rock wall ditches in and around Bladensburg. Now a suburb of Washington, D.C., Bladensburg, Maryland, was then a small commercial town—Washington did not exist.

Henry joined the Maryland Line during the revolution, and served under General Washington at the Battle of Brandywine. In that fight, Henry was among members of the Maryland Line captured by the British. Henry was put on a ship and sent to Jamaica, where he was made to labor on a sugar plantation. A year later, the British moved Henry to West Florida and more slave labor on another sugar plantation. He escaped, walked across Florida to a Spanish colony, and got himself on a boat headed north to Philadelphia.

In Philadelphia, Henry learned that General Washington had gone south to Virginia. While Lord Cornwallis was surrendering to General

---

From *History of Johnson County, Vol. II*, Johnson County (Tennessee) Historical Society, 2000. Joe Wilson wrote: "This was written in 1998 for a book being prepared by the Johnson County Genealogical Society. The Main family were neighbors and good friends of my family at Trade."

Washington at Yorktown, assuring American independence, Henry Main was a few miles out of the little town, walking toward his place of duty in Washington's army.

Back in Bladensburg, after the war, Henry married a widow: Elizabeth Berry Ford. Her husband had died in the Revolution and left her with two children. Elizabeth and Henry had one child of their own: Charles Main, born in 1788.

Charles was a babe in arms when Henry and Elizabeth joined an exodus from Maryland to North Carolina (where they lived near members of the Greer family, which also came south in this period). Henry left Maryland as soon as the grass was up in the spring, driving the family livestock before him. Elizabeth left two or three weeks later, driving a wagon with the children and some household goods, in company with others traveling south. They had planned to meet in the Wilkes County area of North Carolina, then a frontier region. But they became lost from each other, and Elizabeth searched for Henry for a month before she found him. It was an incident so frightening to the family that it was carried in verbal stories among Wilson descendants of the Main family until the 1950s.

Charles Main married Patience Berry and served in the War of 1812. Most members of the Main family (some spelling it Mains or Maine) in Johnson, Watauga, and Ashe counties are descended from Charles and Patience. They had a large family, and lived in each of these counties.

The information here about Henry's military service is largely from his pension claims and records in the National Archives. When asked if anyone could verify his statements, Henry gave the name of his old captain, William Bealle of Bladensburg, and said he could verify, "if living." The captain was living, and told pension officials that Henry's accounts were accurate.

The Main family is associated with the early settlement of Long Hope Mountain, the high plateau on the Ashe and Watauga County border. The late Kay Brown, unofficial historian and keeper of Long Hope stories, had a story about how the mountain got its name. Kay said, "The first old man that lived up there talked funny. If anybody asked why he lived up there, it being so cold and far from everybody, he'd say, 'I'd long hoped to find such a place.' He said 'long hoped to find' so often that Long Hope got to be a joke name and then the real name for the place."

Did the old man who "talked funny" have a British accent, and was he Henry Main? Kay didn't recall a name. At this point there's probably no way to be sure, but an old soldier who had sweated and swatted mosquitoes doing slave labor in Jamaica and West Florida might indeed have "long hoped" to find a place as high, cool, and free as that beautiful spot.

# Grant and Sherman Come to Trade

Well, not really. I have yet to find a shred of evidence that the two top general officers in the U.S. Army during the Civil War ever set foot in Tennessee's easternmost community.

Yet no community in the nation could have named a higher percentage of its sons for the leadership that preserved the Union. When I was a lad, ninety years after the end of "the war" (no other war having the distinction of merely needing a "the" to identify it), there was plentiful evidence of a mighty devotion to the Union in Trade.

Grant Baumgardner lived down the road a quarter mile. Grant Snyder lived a few miles up the road. There was a Grant—and often two or three—in any direction you took. We were equally blessed with citizens named for William Tecumseh Sherman. Sherman Wallace lived down the road, and Sherman Miller over a hill. There were enough Shermans thereabouts to carry the coffin of any mountain farmer who might take his leave of us.

Trade is so deep in the mountain South that white-flint cornbread and creasy greens were almost always part of dinner and supper.

---

Joe Wilson wrote: "This was written in 2011, but never published."

(Anyone confusing "dinner" with an evening meal would have been treated with pity.)

Most places in the South would have then sooner named a son for Beelzebub than Grant or Sherman, but we had a flowering of them, a lingering reminder that the fiercest supporters the American Union had during "the war" were from northeastern Tennessee.

Trade and other communities in Johnson County also named sons for President Lincoln, and—mountain folk being noted for brevity—their names were usually shortened to "Link." So Link Hodge lived up the road, and Link Shoun a little beyond him.

My great-great grandpa Musgrove left a keepsake unusual for Southerners of his time: a beautifully framed photograph of John Brown, the fierce abolitionist hanged for treason by the Commonwealth of Virginia in 1859. Ol' John is staring balefully at the photographer with the burning eyes of a zealot. Did he have a premonition that, within four years, a million men in blue would tramp southward singing, "John Brown's body lies a-moldering in the grave, but his soul goes marching on?"

There's a small mountain of books in which history professors seeking tenure blather on about why the mountain South was loyal. The "Mountain Yankee" cavalrymen who held the stars and stripes aloft are often said to have been concerned about competition from slave labor, but there's not an iota of evidence of that in what local people said at the time.

What is abundantly clear is that they despised slavery, and especially the idea that they could be conscripted and made to fight and die to protect it. It was the Confederate conscription officers who rode in, telling them they must protect ol' Massa's right to never break a sweat while growing rich off the labor of ragamuffin poor people, that sent them en masse into the Union army.

After the war they became Lincoln Republicans, and to this day Republicans control Johnson County. Johnson was the most Republican county in the United States during a part of the 1930s, in the percentage of voters preferring the party.

Though financially strapped throughout their history, northeastern Tennessee Republicans have made accommodations with the business interests that came to the party. When Kansas governor Alf Landon opposed President Roosevelt in 1936 with a promise to repeal Social Security, Johnson County voters preferred Landon by a whopping margin of 86 percent.

Nowadays, Social Security is by far the largest payroll in the region, but Johnson County is still Republican. Most local citizens begin their explanation of personal voting preference with, "My daddy. . . ."

Even now, were it put to a vote, they'd much prefer ol' Massa earn his creasy greens and cornbread by breaking a sweat.

*A native of Trade, Tennessee, Joe Wilson is a registered Democrat.*

# Hanging the Hangman

Joe Wilson wrote:

This has never been published, and is true. I started writing it in 1986, and finally finished it in 2005. The Mountain Yankee story about hanging a Confederate hangman could get you run out of Charleston. Among the many tribes of Southerners, the Mountain Yankees are fully lost in the current welter of Rhett worship. Avoid Charleston. . . .

"Lucky Joe" was well known in his time as an outlaw, and you can still find stories about him on the internet by searching on "Lucky Joe Wilson." A Winston-Salem plug tobacco maker named a form of plug for him, and I have a metal tobacco tag with his name. These were once affixed to each plug, and the chewer sometimes attached these to his barn door or whatever else needed the decoration. I also have a Civil War photo of him as a youth in a Union cavalryman's jacket.

Stories of his exploits were spread by newspapers across the nation, but my Grandpa's older brother Frank Wilson, a teacher (and son of "Lucky Joe") commented, 'Pa would not have had time to do all those things if he had lived to be 200, and he died at 57.' But, of course, Uncle Frank had his own batch of "Lucky Joe" stories, and said they were true.

*"It was jist after they swum the river naked, and hung the hangman"*

I first saw the small marble stone over Jacob May's grave on Decoration Day when I was nine or ten years old. Aunt Stella was making her annual pilgrimage to the Arrendall Cemetery, leaving small offerings of wildflowers at selected graves. Aunt Stella had a handful of deep blue violets, surrounding a single wild red-flecked rose for Jacob. She carefully arranged the violets to frame the rose and stood this bouquet in a tin can of water at the headstone. The bouquet, and a gentle caress she gave the stone as she turned away, told me that Jacob was very special. So I peered at the inscription.

It gave only his name and a military service line: "Co I 13th Tenn. Cav." I knew even then that this referred to a local "Mountain Yankee" cavalry unit that became famous in the Civil War, one that had helped create the "rebellion within the rebellion," a fierce resistance to Confederate authority in northeastern Tennessee. Yet this was not a gravestone issued by the government, like those above Civil War soldiers nearby. It was smaller and much finer.

"Who was he?" I asked Aunt Stella, knowing she could tell about anyone who had lived since pioneer times in this high mountain valley under the looming face of 5,574-foot Snake Mountain in Trade, Tennessee's oldest and easternmost community.

"He was just a boy," she said. "Not much older than you. But the rebels hung him and another boy, and Frank Grayson had to take a horse and sled way down in North Carolina and drag his body home. His mother was an Arrendall, so they washed him and dressed him, and tried to cover the bruises on his face with powder. They prayed and sung some songs, and buried him here. It made his daddy as mad as a hornet, and he came home from that war with a new rifle that would shoot sixteen times. Some bad trouble started here."

Aunt Stella promised to tell more in a day or two, and left me standing transfixed beside a creamy white block of marble in a place where the bloom of spring was turning into summer.

Aunt Stella was not a relative. She lived alone on a tiny farmstead up a hollow near our farm. She had been the teenaged second wife of an older farmer. She had helped him raise children as old as her, and had given him a second younger family. Her husband was the oldest son of a Civil War veteran, so when his parents were old and had to "break up housekeeping," his father came to live with him and Aunt Stella, while his mother went to live with her oldest daughter and her family. So Aunt Stella had known a talkative veteran of the Civil War.

In Aunt Stella's early married years, friends of the old soldier visited almost every weekend, and he fascinated the children with tales about battles fought a generation earlier. His stories about Trade and the turmoil that swept over it were equally interesting to his young daughter-in-law.

Grey moss and brown lichens had been growing over the old soldier's gravestone for two generations. Aunt Stella's husband had long since joined him, and her children and grandchildren lived in various far-distant places. She walked out of her hollow every day, holding carefully to the handrail as she crossed the footbridge over rushing Bulldog Creek. She arrived near noon, after the mailman had passed. He often brought nothing, so she paused before she opened the mailbox and carefully felt inside. Often a pensive shadow crossed her face.

But by the time she had crossed our yard and reached the door of our five-room bungalow, her voice was cheery as she called to my mom, "Josie, can ye stand some company?" She always called out, though she knew her visits were the most important event of the day for Mom and her family.

A handmade rocking chair with pillows was reserved for Aunt Stella, and she easily settled into it, offering to assist with any bean stringing or apple peeling that might be underway. A query from my mother often prompted her first story, and we were suddenly off on a visit to times gone by. She remained for at least three hours, but left before we prepared supper. She spent those hours telling us about neighbors who had once shared these green hills, multi-blue mountains, and rushing creek. We heard about murders that happened four generations earlier, and children that had been carried off by Indians. We heard about marital indiscretions by men, including one fellow who had a wife at Trade and another in Kentucky.

Aunt Stella had no refrigeration, but, after milking, my brother or I took a small crock of milk to her springhouse and stood it in the cool running water of her milk trough. She got a mold of butter when we churned, and when Mom cut a homemade cheese, a chunk was for Aunt Stella. We'd sit on the porch of her little house and hear about people who had once lived in this small farming community on the western side of the Blue Ridge Mountains.

She also told stories to my brother and me when we dragged wood off a ridge for her heating and cooking stoves, using a crosscut saw to cut it into foot-and-a-half lengths. We then split the blocks with a double-bit axe, carefully stacking the firewood on her porch. She sometimes played her pump organ for my brother and me. She knew old ballads and Victorian songs, and encouraged us to sing with her on such songs as "Fair Ellender" and "Sweet Sunny South."

If a lucky day came and I caught what we called "a mess of" trout, the finest and largest one went to Aunt Stella, because she liked trout baked with slivers of white onion, potato, and carrots in an iron baker that sat in the coals of her fireplace. The smell would fill her little house, and she'd tell me how Peter, a follower of Jesus, had been a fisherman, and say that fishing was a blessed thing to do.

Aunt Stella was especially knowledgeable of what she called "that old Silver War," and the hellish difficulties it brought to Trade. Her late husband had been the son of a wagoner for a local federal cavalry company, the 13th Tennessee. The former teamster—who came to live with Aunt Stella—and his fellow veterans, regular visitors, were rich in experience.

Their wide-ranging raids had covered over 5,000 miles, mostly in back-and-forth movements when they served under federal General Stoneman. They had left their homes as refugees and walked the mountaintops to federal training camps in Kentucky or Ohio. At the end of the war, they were among the federal cavalry that chased Jeff Davis from near the Virginia and North Carolina border across three states and into the arms of the 4th Michigan Cavalry, which took charge of him near Irwinsville, Georgia on May 10, 1865.

Aunt Stella especially liked their stories about the exploits of "Lucky Joe," a youthful corporal in the 13th who would sometimes sneak home and bedevil the high-falutin' men of property the Confederates had put in charge of their rebellious county. "If they had a good horse, he'd get it. If they were mean to a federal soldier's family, Dan Ellis or 'Lucky Joe' might shoot them. But 'Lucky Joe' was best at stealing. They said he could steal the shortening out of a ginger cake without cracking the crust."

I liked the "Lucky Joe" stories. He had been gone for many years, but he was my great-grandfather.

Tennessee's three regions were bitterly divided by the war, with its easternmost counties fiercely supporting President Lincoln's efforts to keep the Union. Their adversaries did not come from the other grand divisions of Tennessee. Raiders and renegades came from North Carolina in an unending stream, all intent on drafting men into the Confederate army by enforcing the hated conscription law of the Confederates.

The best supporter of preserving the American union in Tennessee was then William G. "Parson" Brownlow, editor of the *Knoxville Whig* newspaper. He spoke for most of northeastern Tennessee when, before the war, he gave a sardonic response to Jordan Clark, an Arkansas reader who wondered when the influential Brownlow might come out in support of the Confederacy:

> When the sun shines at midnight and the moon by day, when men forget to be selfish, when all the watercourses in America flow upstream . . .
>
> Not so long as there are sects in churches, weeds in gardens, fleas in hog pens, disputes in families, wars among nations, bad men in America . . .
>
> Sometime after the Pope in Rome joins the Methodist Church, after Queen Victoria agrees to be divorced from Prince Albert by a county court in Kansas, when good men cannot go to heaven or bad men to hell.
>
> When all these matters are in their fullness, and even then I will need to ask the Lord why anyone in their right mind would wish to destroy the finest government ever devised by the minds of men.

The dour Parson's youngest son, Jim Brownlow, as colorful as his father, became a colonel in the "Mountain Yankee" 1st Tennessee Cavalry while still a teenager. He later became the youngest general officer in the Union army. He never ordered men into battle but led them, and became famous for his request, "Come on, boys."

Serving under General Sherman, Jim came to the shores of the flooded Chattahoochee River, where a rebel unit on the opposite side impeded his progress. He ordered a group of his men to disrobe and join him in swimming the river, pushing a small barge carrying their rifles and belts, and to attack the rebs in the dark. As his naked men navigated saw briars and brush in approaching the enemy, Jim begged them, "Cuss low, boys, cuss low."

A Confederate, captured by this naked squad, told young Brownlow, "If we'uns had been strong enough to take you'uns, the Confederacy 'ud a hung you all as spies, cause you hain't got no uniforms on."

Aunt Stella had no gentling euphemisms such as "outraged women" for the rape and pillage of mountain women whose husbands had gone through the lines to fight for the Union. It happened, and Aunt Stella told the truth as she heard it. She told of "one of the Pearce girls," a teenager who married a local boy about to sneak through the lines to Kentucky to join the Union army:

> He built them a cabin near his folks, but then he left and a gang of rebel soldiers from North Carolina came and stole everything she had, and upended her, and every one of them took a turn on her. They kept coming back until she was pregnant and showing and his family ran her off.
>
> So she lived in a little cave in the rock cliff down on the Gorge, washed for women, and did what she could. Her husband would not own her when he came home. Women carried things to her to eat when she had that baby in that rock cliff alone, and she and that baby lived. Right after the war, one of her brothers got holt of enough money to send her west to some of their family, and it was over forty years before she came back to see the graves of her mother and father and older sisters.
>
> She had married a fellow from out there, and he had adopted that boy. That little fellow had grown up and started raising walnuts. He had a big English walnut ranch, and they were rich. I asked her if they would ever come back here to stay, and she laughed and looked at me like I had three heads with a big mustache on each one.

Aunt Stella preceded her telling about the hanging of Jacob May by saying how peaceable Trade had once been. "No one ever got hurt around here until they started that old Silver War. People helped each other put their crops out and bring them in. Everybody had hogs running loose, getting fat on chestnuts and acorns. If a man's hog was over on you, you'd drive him over to his owner. Nobody believed that old war was coming here."

How it came still puzzled her generations later. "They would not leave us alone. It was not safe for a man to hoe his corn. A gang would come and hold guns on him and tie him up, and make him walk into North Carolina or over to Bristol to the railroad. He had to go fight for slavery. We didn't have any slaves, but they called our men slackers and shirkers and wanted to force all of them to fight, so rich men could have colored people do their work."

She told of Dave Bower and his wife, Polly, the only slave owners at Trade. "They had four or five colored people and they changed often because his father was a slave trader from Jefferson (North Carolina).

Dave had to leave when the war came, and it was never safe for them to come back."

According to Aunt Stella, the breaking point came when Confederate conscription gangs committed several murders, the most heinous being that of George Dotson, a relative of ours.

> He was your Great-Grandpa Dotson's older brother, and had a wife and two little children. They lived over on Drake's Creek, and Wiley Thomas—who claimed to be a captain—and several others came from North Carolina at night and dragged him out of his house.
>
> He and another boy they were trying to force into the rebel army ran, and they caught them and shot them dead. It was an awful shock, and the men here knew they had to go to into the Union army or be dragged into fighting for something awfully wrong.
>
> Jacob's father, Jefferson May, was one of the men who went to the Union army by walking to Kentucky, along with my father-in-law, and your other great grandpa, "Lucky Joe." They walked to where they were trained, and then came back into Tennessee by way of Nashville. It was a long time until they were in eastern Tennessee, but when little Jacob was hanged, his father was in Jonesboro and he soon knew what had happened.
>
> There was a Shepherd man over there, running a Carolina Home Guard outfit of the Confederate army. Some people over there were mad because people over here were not helping them with their war. It was awfully dangerous to go over there, but teenage boys with horses have no fear.
>
> Little Jake and Canada Guy were running around together, just two boys riding farm horses, going visiting. They were over in North Carolina on the North Fork, and rebel people over there claimed they were stealing and threatening people. They may have been a little high-spirited, and the Guy family was a little rough, but nobody here ever believed they did anything wrong. They'd gone over there to see girls. If they deserved any punishment, it was a spanking, not to be killed by a bunch of crazy people.
>
> So they caught little Jake and Can Guy, and took them twenty miles down in North Carolina to Warrensville, and hung them on a hill above a store on the (New) river. There was no trial. They never intended to have a trial. They took them down there to get away from anyone here seeing who did it. They could kill them, so they did.

The home guards over there were awful mad at the Guy family, and also killed two of Canada Guy's brothers and his father. His father was an old man and had never harmed anyone.

Little Jake was too young to be in the army, but the men who were in Jeff's company took up a collection to buy that monument that is on his grave. They came here and put it up, and prayed and sung for him.

Jacob's mother came out there to the graveyard early every Sunday morning for the rest of her life, and sat beside his grave for an hour or longer. It was hard on her. Jacob was a good boy. In the winter he'd help his mother with quilting, and before she died, years later, she asked that her body be wrapped for burial in a quilt she and Jacob had made.

Jefferson May come home from the war when he heard his boy had been hung. He took his wife up there to the graveyard and screamed and cried, and swore he'd not eat a bite until he found the man that hung their boy and killed him.

He had a new rifle that would shoot sixteen times, the first repeating rifle ever around here. He had two pistols and a good horse, and friends who were as mad at the bushwhackers as he was. One of them was Reuben Dotson, your great grandpa's brother. Wiley Thomas and others of the same gang had butchered their oldest brother George, so Reuben was mighty hot about that.

People over here knew that Shepherd was going with Amanda Snyder, and her family lived over on the mountain between the Wallace Settlement in Tennessee and Brushy Fork in North Carolina. She was young—no more than sixteen—but girls married young back then. Her family was letting Shepherd come to their house to spark her, and having parties for him. Jeff May and Reuben found out about that and made them a plan.

Shepherd was a fiddler, and had been playing the fiddle there one cold winter night after Christmas, and they had been roasting chestnuts in the fireplace. They filled up his pockets with hot chestnuts before he rode off around midnight. Jeff and Reuben and others were waiting in a dark hemlock grove by the road. They said it was the coldest night in years, and a skiff of blue snow was falling.

Shepherd gave up as soon as they came into the road. I guess he saw they were not little boys, even in the dark. "Gentlemen, I surrender." He must have expected them to parole him back into the Confederate army.

It scared him when he found out he was in the hands of Jeff May. He begged for his life, and blamed the hanging of the children on the people down at Warrensville. He claimed he was taking them to the jail in Jefferson, and people came out in the road and took them away from him.

But it was not a time for talking. Jeff made a hangman's noose, put it around his neck, and threw it over a limb that hung over the road. It was hard to get good rope then, and when he drove the horse from under Shepherd, the rope broke and dropped him in the road.

Jeff got a short stick and took the bridle reins off his horse and put them around Shepherd's neck. He used that stick to twist the bridle reins tight. They'd taken Shepherd's coat off, and Reuben had the coat. So as Jeff twisted and Shepherd yelled, cried and choked and died, Reuben Dotson sat easy in his saddle and eat up his chestnuts.

People make an awful mistake when they get so hot about their politics that they want to kill people who do not agree with them. And when they start killing children, they are liable to end up choking and dying and going to hell in a skiff of blue snow with somebody eating their chestnuts.

# The Visitor

A kid remembers rejection. When I was a kid at Trade, days blended into a seamless mass of learning, exploring, working in the fields, and fishing for trout.

But a kid recalls all the details of rejection. I'm sure I remember the tall visitor in the good leather coat so well because I was rejected twice that day.

It was a cold, snowy day and we were standing in the woodshed when my dad told me to go into the house so he could talk with Uncle Bob Thomas and a visiting stranger.

"We don't need you out here, son," he said.

I was surprised and hurt. I'd listened to Uncle Bob and Dad talk many times and enjoyed it. This was before many people at Trade had cars or pickup trucks, and Uncle Bob walked by once or twice a week.

He and Dad usually talked a few minutes, but sometimes their talk went on for an hour. Uncle Bob said funny things and he liked kids.

---

Unpublished and undated. Joe Wilson wrote: "This story from Trade is about revenge and redemption and is true."

They often talked stock market prices. Their stock market was not the one on Wall Street in New York. Their stock market was in nearby Abingdon and sold cows, calves, steers, bulls, mules, horses, and an occasional herd of sheep. A penny per pound change in price would be noted, and each knew if he was helped or hurt.

Sometimes they talked politics. They were more interested in who wanted to be county superintendent of roads than who wanted to be president.

Listening to Uncle Bob and Dad talk was more entertaining than the winter work of sawing and splitting wood, clearing rocks from the fields, or feeding the cattle.

They didn't care much for new young preachers who talked too long. They agreed that the county agricultural agent didn't know much about farming. One could learn to distrust experts by listening to Dad and Uncle Bob talk about preachers and county agents.

Uncle Bob was not related to us. The "uncle" was an honorific title, respect for a senior.

But on this day, Uncle Bob had arrived in a new car driven by a stranger, an older man with sparkling eyes and a cheerful grin. The car had a license plate from a distant place. It had stickers on the windows. Cars from Trade didn't have stickers, and all were well-used before anyone at Trade could afford them.

Dad greeted the visitor warmly, but I don't recall him speaking his name. The visitor asked my name and if I was named for "Lucky Joe," my outlaw great-grandfather. There are lots of good stories about "Lucky Joe's" escapades, so they laughed.

My dad said I was named for brother Joe, his older brother who died two years before I was born. But he said his brother was named for "Lucky Joe," so perhaps I was too.

I was struck by the visitor's voice. He didn't sound like people from Trade. Yet he knew people from Trade, people from long ago.

I'd expected Dad to take Uncle Bob and the visitor to the living room where the purring Warm Morning wood stove was located, but they went around the house to the woodshed.

People who wanted Dad to go to the barn or woodshed usually had some liquor to offer him. Uncle Bob usually did some drinking after selling his tobacco, but neither he nor the visitor had been drinking that day.

Moreover, Dad had a serious expression. He liked the visitor, but I sensed they were not going to talk about the stock market or who was going to run for road superintendent.

It was when we arrived at the woodshed that Dad sent me to the house. After his abrupt, "We don't need you out here, Son!" I looked hesitant, and he added, "Go on!" and pointed to the kitchen door. The visitor noted my disappointment and pressed a dime into my hand. "You're a good boy, Little Joe," he said. It was the first money I'd received for doing nothing, and I was glad to get it. But I'd have rather stayed and heard them talk.

I watched from the kitchen window as they talked in the winter chill, sometimes stamping to keep their feet warm, their forms outlined in the archway of the woodshed for an hour as darkness fell.

I experienced rejection again when the visitor and Uncle Bob drove off, and Dad came into the house to warm himself.

"Dad, who was that?' I asked.

"Son, you don't need to know who that was, and I don't want you talking about Bob being here with somebody you didn't know. We're not going to say anything about this. Is that clear?" His voice was stern.

Dad had never said anything like that before, and he never did again.

It was ten years later when Chief Green told us about the worst murder that ever happened. A group of boys and a few older loafers had gathered at the corner of Church and Main in Mountain City on Saturday night. The only traffic light in our county was located there. We were discussing a recent murder when an evaluation was requested from the chief, a retired former Mountain City policeman. "Chief, that must have been the worst thing that ever happened around here," someone opined.

The comment invited a comparison. A bad murder could be far from the worst. Ranking tragedies was easier in those years, before television began reporting a murder every night just before the weather.

The comment was addressed to the right person. Chief had many years of law enforcement experience. He'd sat by the stove in county jails on long nights and heard about the gory deeds of heartless killers.

Chief recalled a tragedy from forty years earlier. "Worst thing that ever happened around here was the killing of Lilly Thomas," he said.

The chief said Lilly was an attractive girl in her mid teens who became interested in a neighbor in his twenties. The neighbor had a farm across a ridge from the Thomas homestead in the North Fork community, a few miles south of Trade in North Carolina.

The neighbor also had a wife and children, but he asked Lilly to meet him in the woods. No one knew how long or often they met, but Lilly became pregnant.

Her lover told Lilly he would obtain a machine that would make the baby be absorbed back into her body so she would no longer be pregnant.

He brought her a large canvas belt packed with long cylinders. He told Lilly that she should go alone into the high woods and strap the heavy belt around her. Then she should light a fuse attached to the belt. A smoke would come from the belt and she should inhale it. It might make her cough a little, but it would end the pregnancy without harming her.

Her lover made Lilly promise not to tell anyone, but Lilly had already told her girlfriend about her lover and her condition. Her friend went part way to the high woods with Lilly.

But Lilly felt so strongly about her promise to her lover that she made her friend wait on a lower ridge while she lit the fuse, alone on a high ridge as she had promised.

The dynamite in the belt blew pieces of Lilly into the treetops. Chief was then a small boy, good at climbing, and he told of climbing trees to retrieve bits of Lilly and her clothing.

There was a trial, of course. Lilly's girlfriend told what she knew. Her murderer denied any involvement with the pretty teenager. His family was considered a good one and they had money. The skills needed to pervert justice were for sale in the Appalachian mountains then, as they are now everywhere in America. His lawyers were excellent and the jury acquitted him.

But chief said the matter did not end there. He said Lilly had two brothers, Bob and Charlie, both near her age. "Some of you may know Bob," he said. "That's Uncle Bob, up at Trade."

The Thomas brothers let it be known they would avenge their sister. The neighbor charged Charlie Thomas with threatening him, and a court placed Charlie under a peace bond.

The neighbor went armed and carefully avoided the young Thomas brothers for a year, but the inevitable happened.

He was at a gristmill when Charlie Thomas drove up with a wagon loaded with corn. The neighbor decided that he'd done enough avoiding, that it was time to stand his ground with the teenager. It was his last mistake. Charlie was lifting a shotgun from behind the wagon seat.

Chief said Charlie hurried home and his family took him to Johnson City, where he boarded a train for the West. He said no one did much to persuade Western authorities to find the brother who had avenged his sister.

Chief said Charlie never came back, "and I'm glad he has not, because I'd have to arrest him."

It was a warm night, but a cold chill gave me goose bumps. I suddenly knew the name of the stranger who gave me a dime and talked in the archway of our woodshed as darkness fell on Trade on a snowy day.

But I didn't tell the chief or anyone else about a car with stickers and a California license plate. I kept the secret my father didn't tell me.

# Technology Comes to Trade

We have at times resisted new technology at Trade. My dad told of the fierce resistance one of our neighbors offered when told he must build an outhouse.

It was during the Great Depression, and there was good reason in those days before indoor plumbing to own what was sometimes called "a necessary house." The reason was far more than odors and the "oh-my-god" mishaps the absence of one might cause.

Typhoid was endemic, and it is a water-borne disease. It had killed hundreds of thousands of Americans over the generations, and could be largely stopped by nothing more complicated than better sanitation and devices as simple as the humble outhouse.

Roundworms were also endemic and spread by human waste drying in open air. Tapeworm was less common but caused by what my mom called "old ordinary nastiness."

---

Unpublished and undated. Joe Wilson wrote: "Located in a gap in the Blue Ridge Mountains, Trade is the easternmost and oldest community in Tennessee. The people who live in Trade raise tobacco and work in a few nearby light industry plants. Tobacco is not doing well, and some of the plants are moving to Asia and Mexico."

Thousands needed work, and among the most far-sighted programs of the Works Progress Administration of the Franklin Roosevelt administration was one that promoted the building of outhouses. Of course, this good and inexpensive public health solution for the poor was greeted with jeering by guardians of the public purse in Congress. Stale poo-poo jokes were dusted off, and class warfare reached new lows.

But Roosevelt's men were not easily deterred and were willing to use the powers of government to insure compliance with health regulations. So our neighbor at Trade was told he had no choice—he had to own an outhouse for the use of his family.

That he could not afford to pay for one was easily countered. He could work for WPA for three days, building outhouses for others, and be rewarded by a fine one that would be built for him.

It would resemble thousands of others built across the nation. A pit six feet deep would be dug, and the throne would be positioned on a concrete slab over it. The walls would be one-inch boards, and a shed roof would protect it from rain and snow. Burnt lime would be provided, and a handful tossed into the pit occasionally would make the enterprise very successful and comfortable.

Our contrarian neighbor had a final question. "You certain I got to do this?"

"Yes."

"Well, by God, they may be able to make me build it, but they can't make me use it."

His resistance was discussed with glee and approval by the loafers holding down the store porch at the Trade general store, but within weeks the outhouse was itself a pillar of the country joke.

An early knee-slapper from those days still circulates. It tells of a lad who turned over an outhouse. His father sternly accosted him, "Son, did you turn over our outhouse?"

"Father, I cannot tell a lie. I turned that sucker over."

The father hitches up his britches and begins removing his broad leather belt, obviously intent on warming the butt of his miscreant son.

"But Dad, when George Washington cut down the cherry tree and told the truth, his father didn't whip him."

"That's right, Son. But George Washington's father was not in that cherry tree."

My father could laugh at dumb-ass resistance to sanitation regulations, but his own faith-based resistance to technology was at least as obdurate as that of the neighbor. When I obtained a job with an airline, flying around the country, building parts depots for the first turboprops, he was appalled. Members of our family had never flown, and he was concerned and asked me to sit with him for a serious discussion.

"Son, if the Lord had intended for man to fly, he'd have been born with wings."

"Dad, if he'd intended for us to roll around on wheels, would we have been born on roller skates?"

Faith does not bow to logic, and no expression of the perfectly obvious ever convinced my father. He and many others saw human existence while spiritually standing on the Temple Mount in old Jerusalem.

So Dad gave his usual response: "Son, you are in darkness."

Among the difficulties of embracing technology is that it can become prematurely stretched beyond its belts and gears, diodes and transistors, to a belief system. Some believe because it works, in a world where much that is inherited tradition does not. Yet one must be careful in attributions.

The flutter mill works, but grinds no corn.

That the medium is the message is a glittering insight that came to the nation's media professors in the 1960s, but it came to Trade voyeurs forty years earlier when radio was introduced.

Nothing like radio had happened before, and the nation was almost instantly obsessed by popular culture. It mesmerized people in cities more than it did folk at Trade. President Coolidge let it be known that he could not be disturbed during broadcasts of the *Amos and Andy Show*, a blackface minstrel-based sitcom that followed two black men blundering their way along a life path strewn with hilarious mishaps.

Among other benefits, it assured white men of their superiority. They were too smart to be felled by the snares and tomfoolery that brought down Amos and Andy.

But radio was more than popular entertainment. It announced the end of the old order and shrunk the world in startling ways. It seemed like magic; the future had arrived. The president could speak to you, and all the greatest musical artists could be heard. In the early static-free years, one could hear an announcer's intake of breath or the crumpling of paper a thousand miles away.

Tip Madron brought the first radio to Trade, a battery-powered black box with a separate horn that often blared all day and much of the night. Tip's ample living room was packed with visitors almost every evening, and he was forced to declare 10:00 p.m. as turn-off time.

The July 2, 1921, Jack Dempsey and Georges Carpentier World Champion boxing match created a major babble of excitement at Trade. Johnson County men had been to France recently, in World War I, and had huge affection for this ally. One of them, Conley Powell, had named a baby daughter Paris France Powell, reasoning she was the prettiest thing he had seen since he was a doughboy in Paris (and she did grow up to be a truly lovely lady).

Carpentier was a war hero, while Dempsey was considered a draft dodger. This hugely promoted extravaganza drew a record 90,000 to an outdoor arena, and was the first sports event to ever be described on radio.

Even a half-century later, retired mail carrier Uncle Tip had vivid memories of those who gathered at his house to hear the radio broadcast. "So many people had said they were coming, that I had to move the radio out on the porch. I could turn the volume up and a big crowd standing in the yard could hear."

But after the very aggressive Dempsey began pounding his opponent, a visitor Uncle Tip described as "an old fellow from over in Beaver Dams" became agitated, and rushed over to Uncle Tip.

"Tip, if you don't turn that dang thing off, he's a-going to kill that feller."

The assessment was prescient. Dempsey knocked Carpentier unconscious after one minute and sixteen seconds of the fourth round, after just eleven minutes of fighting.

Death and danger were associated with other technology as it seeped into Trade. Railroads built around 1900 to remove the giant stands of virgin timber were soon immortalized in "take warning" ballads. An early lyric warns about the strangers who came with the railroad:

> A railroad man will kill you if he can
> And drink your blood like wine.

But railroad engineers and firemen were soon viewed as heroes who endured danger and loved pretty girls. Train wrecks became a major topic for tragedy ballads. Henry Whitter's song, "The Wreck of the Southern Old 97," was among the first hit phonograph recordings of hillbilly music. Whitter was admired at Trade as a partner of Johnson County's great fiddler and singer, G.B. Grayson. Whitter's lyric told the wreck story:

He was going down grade
Making 90 mile an hour
When his whistle begin to scream.
He was found in that wreck,
With his hands on the throttle,
And was scalded to death with the steam.

But while songs about murder, major wrecks, and other calamities were commonplace, songs that made jokes of morbid obsessions about disaster were equally common. The "answer song" for "The Wreck of the Old 97" proclaimed:

She was going down town,
Making forty miles an hour,
When the sprocket on her bicycle broke.
She was found in the grass,
With the sprocket up her ass,
Tickled to death by the spokes.

At Trade, a traditional wish for balance between the very serious and uproariously funny extends even to views about ministers of the gospel. Trade and other tiny places in the Blue Ridge tend to have an oversupply of hellfire and brimstone preachers, but are also beautifully supplied with good preacher jokes.

These jokes continue even today, and one from twenty years ago shows their continuous updating. It is concerned with evangelist Billy Graham, long a resident of the Asheville area, and since 1950 viewed almost as a saint by many at Trade's Evergreen Baptist Church.

In the story, Billy is returning home via Charlotte's Douglas International Airport. He muses about his generations of travel and those who have assisted him and decides it would be good to honor the faithful chauffeur who always awaits him near the gate.

"I'm going to drive you tonight," he tells the chauffeur. "This time you can relax, and I'll drive you home." The surprised chauffeur protests, but Graham cannot be dissuaded. He climbs into the chauffeur's seat while his employee takes Graham's usual place. Graham roars off up the Billy Graham Parkway, and fails to take heed of the speed limit. Suddenly there is a siren and blue lights.

Graham finds his driver's license and registration, and the rookie highway patrolman walks back to his patrol car and calls his sergeant.

"I think I've done it again," he blurts to the sergeant.

"What, you've stopped the mayor again?"

"No, it is worse than that!"

"Good Lord, dude, you've stopped the governor?"

"No, I don't know who it is, but it must be the Pope or Jesus Christ. He's got Billy Graham driving him!"

Laughing at technology and its warping of tradition is a way to tame its demands and control its intrusions. Turning the radio off and humanizing the great media preacher are small but useful steps.

The coming of the automobile and its innovations has entertained residents of Trade for over a century. A story concerning the naming of the "Molly turn" on one of the now abandoned roads to Mountain City tells of a poignant moment in this history.

A "turn" is a wagoner's term for a curve. This one was named for a mishap that befell Miss Molly, the beloved belle of the Bulldog community, when she attempted to navigate it while waving to friends from an early Oldsmobile.

Cars were new and Miss Molly was an inexperienced driver. She had often passed the Wilson farm with her fine buggy and trotter, gaily waving at the Wilson girls and boys.

But this day, Molly came chugging down the road with a friend in a new high-wheel 1907 Oldsmobile convertible coupe. The top was down, and beautiful Miss Molly sat tall above a steering stick that reached no higher than her waistline. She was helloing, waving, and holding onto a wide-brimmed flat hat with flowers and a bow. Her skirt reached to her feet and was blowing in the breeze.

Molly managed the left turn from the Bulldog Road onto what became an early version of Highway 421. Roan's Creek had been flooded by an early morning rain, and was deep and muddy. The road was some twenty feet above the creek and as Molly approached the turn, the Wilson youngsters ran across bottomland, eager to see her car.

Busy tending her skirt, holding her hat, and waving at the Wilsons, Molly forgot to steer into the turn. The car began a slow left flip into the creek. The passenger managed to leap to safety, but beautiful Molly had no such luck.

Eighty years later, Inez Wilson told of the commotion. "That car turned completely upside down, but Molly went climbing up it, and it somehow flipped her beyond it. She was tall and slender and her feet were over her head, and she went into the creek headfirst, upstream from the car. You could see the red ruffles on her drawers as she dived straight in and went swimming in that muddy water with the bullfrogs, mud turtles, and muskrats."

Miss Molly was crestfallen but uninjured, and the Reece boys soon had the car running again. But the curve was named in her honor, and to this day descendants of the Wilson family know it as "the Molly turn."

Molly's flip into the creek may have been the most memorable accident on that stretch of old Highway 421, but it is also known for a major misconception that took place in 1953. A neighbor we shall call Henry had walked out of the Bulldog community and waited by the road for the offer of a ride to Mountain City.

A Zionsville lad who had been working for Chrysler in Detroit soon gave him a ride. This fellow had brought home a fine new Chrysler Imperial with a new innovation: air conditioning. It was a warm day in early October; this was the first air conditioning anyone had seen at Trade, and he had it on full blast.

Hog killing time at Trade comes later, in mid-November or later, when "hard freeze" weather has killed most insects and meat can be protected from their depredations. This was two months before hog killing time, but, as they traveled on toward Mountain City, Henry shivered in the blast of the air conditioner. "By durn it has turned off cold," he said. "I think I'll kill my hogs tomorrow."

Keeping track of the rhythms of life and matters as elemental as food preservation by temperature had preceded European settlement at Trade. But the larger change was that one could go to a distant place and transfer the rewards of work back home.

Increases in the prices of burley tobacco and the selling of snap beans brought new prosperity to Trade in 1950 and the years that followed.

Technology reached toward the farm. Many who had never owned cars bought their first one.

Suddenly, all the hillside farmers at Trade had pickup trucks. Uncle John Wallace had one of the better farms—but no truck. His son Bert had a good one, but Uncle John was noted for having the best of everything.

He bided his time, figuring out which course was best for him. He then went to the Chevrolet place in Mountain City and bought a baby blue 1953 Bel Air four-door sedan. It had an automatic transmission for ease of driving—the first at Trade. It was beautiful: with fender skirts, a purring Hollywood muffler, a windshield shade, and the best radio.

Uncle John was a skilled horseman and had always had the best teams and riding horses in Trade. But he could not drive. Word came that Bert would be giving him driving lessons next Sunday. We'd been watching older owners master the clutch and other intricacies of driving, and had seen moments as exciting and funny as a bucking horse show. Sensing the possibility of some ridiculous scenes, the boys assembled after Sunday dinner ("lunch" if you are a Yankee) on the bank of the road above Uncle John's fine acreage.

Soon the baby blue Chevrolet came purring slowly down the lane from the farmhouse. Bert was on the passenger side and Uncle John was driving, wearing his bifocals, his white Stetson set level on his grizzled head, both hands gripping the wheel, staring straight ahead.

Uncle John had fine gates, built of the best white oak, stove-bolted together, painted deep red, and kept level by a cable that extended at an angle from the pivoting post. They were the most attractive and strongest gates at Trade.

We waited for him to apply the brakes at the gate, but he never did. The Chevrolet burst through the gate in a great splintering of timber and crashing and banging of metal, with Uncle John shouting, "Whoa, goddamn you, whoa! Whoa! WHOA!"

We slunk away, not wishing for Uncle John to know we had witnessed his driving shame, when he walked back to his home. The car was soon repaired, but it was Uncle John's last driving lesson.

The miracle of telephone communication has been in a state of furious improvement since the 1890s, but always in the direction of continuous blather. Alexander Bell's invention is the undisputed champion tool of time wasting, and continues in that role. Trade has probably made fewer contributions to its uselessness than Syracuse, but has had its interesting moments.

The telephone also came to Trade in the twenties. These were party lines, with as many as ten families on a single line. Trade was suddenly connected to the nation, but privacy was not part of the package. One could listen in, and many did.

Lucille was a constant listener on Bulldog Road, and often summoned help for neighbors when it was needed. She heard about the runt bear almost as soon as it was spotted on upper Bulldog.

Bears are now commonplace at Trade, but were extinct from around 1900 until 1980. A bear might occasionally stray from the Great Smoky Mountain National Park, but this was rare. Yet our ancestors had been bear hunters, and bear hunting stories continued to be told. Like other stories, these became exaggerated as they were handed on. By the time the stories came to us, the bear had become a man killer.

Of course this was silly; the eastern black bear is only a hungry opportunist. But Lucille and others at Trade did not know this in the mid-forties. Soon several pickup trucks were buzzing up the Bulldog Road, loaded with shotgun-wielding residents.

Our good neighbor Carl and his dad shot the runt bear, tied it onto the back of a '36 Ford, and drove it to the schools at Trade. We saw it first at the two-room Glendale School on Bulldog, but they also took it to the three-room Trade School, and the one-room Wallace School. It was a considerable educational opportunity, and a portion of the education was for Carl and his father as they encountered the Tennessee game warden upon their return.

The warden did not regard the runt bear as a danger and charged Carl and his father with killing a bear out of season. They were fined $75, then a month's wage at Trade. One could get a rise from Carl a generation later by asking, "Been bear hunting lately?"

Anything said on a telephone from Trade was instantly known to the community, and contributed to the quality of gossip. Young lovers devised code words for use on the telephone. Places were given numbers and a new language developed.

The complications of serving business clients and gossipmongers sometimes roiled relations for the telephone company in Mountain City. An energetic fellow we shall call Johnny owned the best garage for repairing or servicing pickup trucks. The county had no warehouse with an inventory of parts, so Johnny telephoned his supplier in Johnson City, who sent the parts by the next bus.

One called Central to place a long distance call. Central was upstairs over a furniture store in Mountain City, with ladies in flowery dresses using equipment Bell himself may have designed. The manager wore a three-piece suit, and his Victorian aplomb and petty brusqueness told that the telephone monopoly was highly respectable.

There were only a few lines to Johnson City, and Johnny was having difficulty getting to his supplier before the afternoon bus departed. After his third attempt, the operator assisting him sent a shot over his bow: "Johnny, some of the girls are talking to friends in Johnson City, and you may just have to stop bothering us and place this call tomorrow."

Johnny returned the shot before he hung up: "Operator, how about sticking this telephone up your ass?"

The manager, in a three-piece suit, came calling within minutes. "Johnny, we do not allow anyone to be rude to our operators. If you do not call our operator and apologize today, we will have to take your telephone out."

Johnny was incredulous. "You'd take my telephone out?" Assured that this action was now pending, Johnny called central. "Are you the operator I told to stick the telephone up her ass?"

"You are?"

"Well, you had better get ready, because they are bringing it in!"

There are many other stories from Trade, and the cornucopia of constantly arriving new gadgets insures our maladjustment to the newfangled will never end. At one point, we used a homemade corn product to lubricate our discussions of such matters, but that was before the hippie boys brought seeds for a weed that has wrapped such discussions in a blue haze.

Joe's great-grandfather, "Lucky Joe" Wilson, late in the 19th century.

*Left to right:* Joe (babe in arms), James Wilson (father), Kenneth Wilson (older brother), Josephine Wilson (mother).

Joe in elementary school.

Joe as a student at Mountain City High School, 1954. He is in the second to last seated row, second from the aisle, wearing a light-colored shirt, an undershirt, and a flat-top haircut.

Joe with his high school band, the Country Cousins.

1980, Rangoon, Burma (now Yangon, Myanmar). *Left to right:* D. L. Menard, Jerry Douglas, Buck White, John Jackson, Cheryl White, Al McKenney, Joe Wilson, and Sharon White (now Skaggs). The remaining three individuals are unknown.

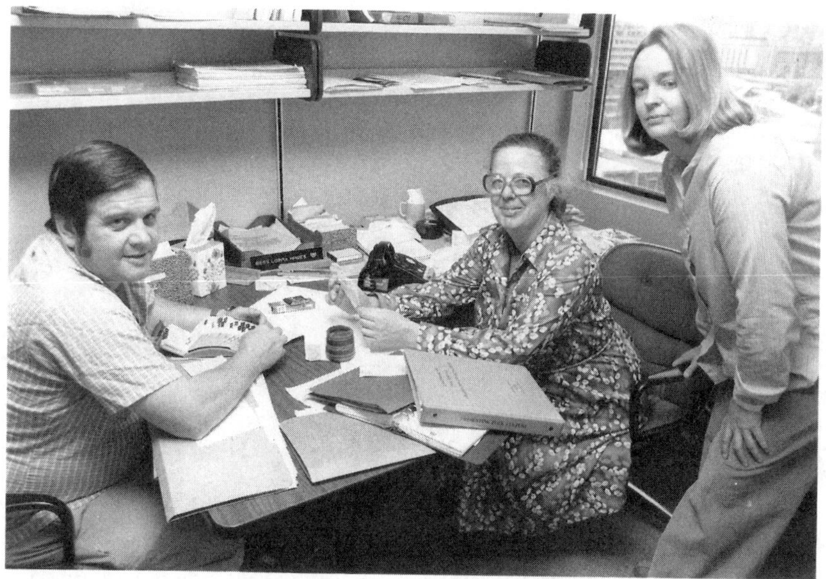

1984 or slightly earlier. *Left to right:* Joe Wilson, Bess Lomax Hawes, and intern Gloria Throne at the National Endowment for the Arts.

Joe under the van on the cowboy tour, 1983.

Joe lobbying in Washington, October, 1996. *Left to right:* Joe Wilson, Keith Kennedy (staff director of the Senate Appropriations Committee), Winston Tabb (Assistant Librarian of Congress) at a party at the Library of Congress celebrating the reauthorization of the American Folklife Center for two years. The LOC had wished to make it a LOC department. Joe and Keith (with the help of Congressman Dave Obey (D-Wisconsin) turned it around. Tabb was on the other side.

Group portrait of Virginia-born or resident National Heritage Fellows, 2007. *Left to right:* Barry Bergey (Director, Folk and Traditional Arts, National Endowment for the Arts); John Cephas, Wayne Henderson, Flory Jagoda, Jesse McReynolds, Ralph Stanley, and Joe Wilson. (Photo by Tom Pitch.)

Joe with his wife Kathy James (center) and stepdaughter Jackie Pfeffer (left) at the presentation of his Living Legend Award from the Library of Congress, September 2009.

A compelling portrait of Joe at the end of his life. (Photo by Pat Jarrett, Viginia Foundation for the Humanities)

# CIVIL RIGHTS

# Hucksters of Hate—Nazi Style

*with Edward Harris*

Slightly abridged from *The Progressive*, Volume 28, Number 6, June 1964. In an October 14, 2013, interview with Laura Anderson for the Birmingham Civil Rights Institute Oral History Project, Joe Wilson said:

W. Edward Harris co-wrote with me the headline article on the cover of the June 1964 issue of *The Progressive*. I was not responsible for the title "Hucksters of Hate—Nazi Style," although it was true enough. It was about the National States Rights Party; they were a Ku Klux Klan front.

Ed Harris was raised in Birmingham, and he was a Unitarian like me. I met him when he was an assistant to George Huddleston, the U.S. Congressman from Alabama. He lost his job when Huddleston lost his job, and he came over and sold furniture on Second Avenue to keep body and soul together. He had a house across the street from me on the south side, and in his book [*Miracle in Birmingham: A Civil Rights Memoir*, Stonework Press, 2004] he mentions me and that I had never taken the non-violence pledge.

The lawyers for *The Progressive* were certain that they would be sued for identifying anybody as having been anywhere close to the bombings. They'd apparently been sued before, but they really had the heebie jeebies about it. The editor, Morris Rubin, was a hell of a nice guy. I sent him a copy of the States Rights Party's republished Jewish ritual murder edition of *Der Stürmer*, one of the meanest canards against the Jews. Of course that goes way the hell back, but even in Germany in the

'30s that level of anti-Semitism was considered low class. That damned thing was thick—they published the original journal in the original German. When I sent him a copy of that, it took care of everything; he understood where I was coming from and what these people were.

The only mistake I think that I made in there is that I overestimated the size of the organization. Ed Harris helped me write it, but all of the statistics were my estimate. I don't think there was ever more than a few hundred people that were involved in that in Birmingham.

*The National States Rights Party (NSRP) with its anti-Semitic, anti-Negro, and anti-foreign doctrines is unknown to most Americans. It has been flourishing in spite of the lack of national or even regional attention. With the struggle for civil rights approaching the crisis stage, it is more important than ever that the public become aware of the dangerous potential of the NSRP. As far as we know, this documented, full-length report on the party is the first to appear in any magazine. The authors, Edward Harris and Joseph Wilson, are Alabama freelance writers who have studied the NSRP at close range.*—THE EDITORS.

"Eight, six, four, two
Albert Boutwell is a Jew."

Throughout one week last September, hundreds of teenagers raced through the streets of Birmingham, Alabama, screaming this rhyme about Methodist Mayor Albert Boutwell as if it were a football cheer. Their words were shrieked in contempt in a city seething with racial turmoil. To understand the chilling cry that accompanied the opening of schools, it is necessary to understand the organization that taught these Alabama teenagers to emulate the Hitler Youth: the National States Rights Party, which has adopted the lightning bolt insignia originally symbolizing the *Hitlerjugend*.

The National States Rights Party, which emerged from a coalition of the States Rights Party and the United White Party, was organized at Knoxville, Tennessee, in 1958. Both of the organizations from which the NSRP derived were splinter action groups, short of membership and cash but with great reserves of redneck anti-Semitism, anti-Negroism, and a strong undercurrent of Klan-type anti-Catholicism. The States Rights group that bolted the Democratic Party in 1948 to support South Carolina's Governor [later Senator] Strom Thurmond for president was not involved in the birth of the new party.

The founder of NSRP six years ago was a retired Knoxville salesman, Ned Dupes. The first party headquarters was set up in Jefferson, Indiana, and the party began merging other small third-party movements into its membership. The party first received national attention when the chairman of its Atlanta branch and four other members were arrested and charged with the bombing of an Atlanta synagogue on October 12, 1958, with damage estimated at $200,000. The defendants were acquitted for lack of evidence. The party newspaper commented that, "the Atlanta case was a triumph of concerted effort by the NSRP with allied patriotic groups."

National headquarters were moved to Louisville, Kentucky, and later to Atlanta, Georgia. Both moves backfired when each city successively met its school desegregation crisis with skillful planning that prevented riots or racial chaos. The party now has learned that strong hostility to civil rights gains is the soil in which membership grows; any show of interracial unity in a community is enough to send the NSRP packing. Thus it was that headquarters of the NSRP finally were established in Birmingham in 1961, after party leaders decided this community would be more receptive to its ideas. Within two years, conditions in Birmingham had developed in a direction that proved the party leaders had made a correct estimate.

In the days following the 1963 federal court order to desegregate Birmingham schools, its new mayor-council government—which succeeded nearly twenty years of rampant racism in city hall—was determined to maintain peace in the tense, fear-wracked city. There was a resolve on the part of most segments of the population to do nothing that would put Birmingham on the front pages of the world press. However, weeks of Negro demonstrations in May and the concessions that followed had enraged many whites, who were determined that Birmingham should close its schools rather than submit to desegregation.

Into this tense situation stepped the National States Rights Party. It circulated petitions calling for the closing of schools, organized motorcades, mass meetings, protest demonstrations, and trips to Montgomery to call on Alabama's fiercely segregationist governor, George C. Wallace. The NSRP petition campaign garnered 30,000 names, which were presented to representatives of Governor Wallace three days before the scheduled opening of schools on September 3, 1963. The party's leaders met with the governor's chief aides for more than two hours.

Although Wallace closed some Alabama schools that were facing desegregation, he did not close the Birmingham schools. NSRP members—in uniforms reminiscent of the attire of German stormtroopers—charged police lines at two of the city's three affected schools. These uniformed members were part of an elite "Security Guard," supposedly responsible for keeping order at NSRP meetings. Their attire included wide leather belts with shoulder straps, thunderbolt armbands, and collars with insignia. State and local school board officials used these incidents as an excuse to suspend schools. The local leader of the NSRP, Dr. Edward R. Fields, who is also its national information director, organized protest rallies encouraging boycotts of the schools. Riotous motorcades and demonstrations lasted for nearly eight days.

On September 15, 1963, at 9:22 in the morning, a Negro house of worship, the 16th Street Baptist Church, was bombed. Four little girls attending Sunday school classes were killed, and a dozen other children and adults were injured. That afternoon and night, two Negroes were shot to death, one boy by two passing white youths—one an Eagle scout, the other an honor student—about thirty minutes after they had left an NSRP rally. Birmingham had begun to reap the harvest of racial hatred sown over the years.

The day after that bloody Sunday, a federal grand jury indicted eight NSRP members for their part in interfering with the federally ordered desegregation of schools. Months later, the case was dismissed.

According to the party's official publication, *The Thunderbolt,* the "indicted states righters" were defended by Governor Wallace. The publication quotes from the text of a statement attributed to him which says, in part, " . . . the Justice Department and the District Attorney call upon the Grand Jury to indict people who expressed indignation at forced integration by waving a Confederate flag, booing, or catcalling."

On the basis of the grand jury's original indictment, some twenty-six overt acts of "indignation" were committed by one or more of the various defendants. This included rock throwing, urging crowds to cross police lines, assaulting police, and hitting a detective with a brick.

That mass meetings at which NSRP leaders spoke to thousands of white Birmingham teenagers were effective in teaching hate to the young was proven again on the afternoon of November 22, 1963, when some students in classes at West End, Woodlawn, and Ramsay High Schools rose and cheered at the news of the assassination of President Kennedy. One Negro girl, newly integrated into a Birmingham high school, tells of a white boy punching her in the back on that tragic day and taunting, over and over: "Your daddy's dead. Whatcha gonna do now?"

Clancy Lake, news director of Birmingham's radio station WAPI, editorially placed the blame for these events on " . . . our city's most noted hate peddlers, men who preach that Adolf Hitler, the Nazi butcher, was one of the world's great men," and added, "The hate mongers are still at work, peddling their filth on the fringe of recognized groups."

It cannot be said that the National States Rights Party was solely responsible for the outrageous events in Birmingham, but it did exploit the situation until it exploded into violence. A city that had kept racial bigots at the head of its government for twenty years was uniquely ready for Dr. Fields and the National States Rights Party.

But what is the National States Rights Party? Essentially, it represents a homegrown version of Nazi racism. Its patron saint is the Nazi editor of *Der Stürmer,* Julius Streicher. He has been eulogized in the NSRP monthly, *The Thunderbolt.*

The party's platform demands that "white Christian boys never again be sent to fight and die to appease the interests of an alien minority." Streicher—one of eleven Nazis hanged by the Nuremberg tribunal for his part in the murder of six million Jews—is called "the patron saint of world anti-Jewism" in party literature. This is the Streicher who called the Jew "a parasite, an enemy, an evil-doer, a disseminator of diseases, who must be destroyed in the interest of mankind." It was Streicher who indoctrinated German youth so effectively that when addressing 2,000 young people on Christmas, 1936, he asked, "Do you know who the devil is?" His breathlessly listening audience answered, in a roar, "The Jew, the Jew."

The NSRP claims to advance the "white man's viewpoint;" the hero featured in many of its publications is a god-like mythological creature called "Whiteman." The party's basic technique, borrowed from Hitler, is the "big lie." It publishes and distributes some of the most infamous anti-Semitic literature of all time, promoting its sale in *The Thunderbolt*. Among publications offered for sale by the NSRP and described as "anti-Communist classics" are: *The Protocols of the Elders of Zion*; *Jewish Ritual Murder* by Arnold Leese; *The World Hoax* by Elmer F. Elmhurst; and *The International Jew* by Henry Ford.

The platform of the party calls for complete separation of all non-whites and certain other racial minorities from the White Folk Community. Their "White Folk Community" is never quite spelled out but it is apparently intended to be a paradise free of Negro, Jew, and alien, with everyone "working as a team, placing the greater good of our White Folk Community above any individual or group interest." The party's foreign policy calls for strengthening ties with white nations, ending foreign aid, opposing international agreements, and demanding that white Christian boys never again be sent to fight and die on foreign soil "to appease the Jews."

The NSRP opposes the Ku Klux Klan as a faint-hearted group, Robert Welch of the John Birch Society because he tolerates Jews, Lincoln Rockwell of the American Nazi Party because he is "a tool of the Jews" and represents competition to their group, and rightist groups of all kinds that do not support its anti-Semitism.

While most right-wing and conservative groups idolize Barry Goldwater and dream of his moving into the White House, the NSRP opposes him. The Thunderbolt warns all members not to be misled into supporting "Goldwasser," the party's name for the Arizona senator whom they label a "Kosher Conservative," and the "Judas Goat" senator. Goldwater's part-Jewish ancestry is cited as reason enough to oppose him. David Lawrence, editor of *U.S. News and World Report*, has also been attacked by the NSRP for giving Goldwater a big build-up. The NSRP argues that Lawrence is Jewish and is thus not to be believed. Party leader Fields is suing Lawrence (and the *Birmingham News*, which carries his conservative column) for suggesting that the House Un-American Activities Committee investigate to determine whether the NSRP is getting funds from foreign governments.

The National States Rights Party claims to be the third largest party in America, but this claim is unproven because of its leaders' refusal to divulge statistics. Both party membership and the circulation of *The Thunderbolt* are closely guarded secrets, known only to top echelon leaders. It is known, however, that *The Thunderbolt* press runs have reached 50,000, and that party membership of $5 per year includes a subscription. All fifty states and several foreign countries are represented on the mailing list.

Party literature claims units in thirty-eight states and active units in many large cities. Besides Birmingham, there is some activity in Chicago, New York, Los Angeles, Atlanta, Jacksonville, and Washington, D.C. As far back as 1960—when the NSRP was in its infancy—it was able to muster 500 demonstrators for its cause in Los Angeles alone.

NSRP's financial support comes from memberships, contributions, and sales of books and pamphlets. Its total income figure, like other concrete statistics, is kept secret from both reporters and party members outside the ruling circle.

The NSRP has limited its political activity to national elections, with the exception of an almost unnoticed attempt to capture an Alabama congressional seat in 1962. Since its organization in 1958, the NSRP has twice held national nominating conventions. In 1960, it met at Dayton, Ohio, and nominated Arkansas Governor Orval Faubus for the presidency and retired Admiral John G. Crommelin for the vice-presidency. The party managed to get the Faubus/Crommelin ticket on the ballot in Arkansas, Louisiana, Kentucky, Delaware, Tennessee, and Florida—without the help of Governor Faubus, who would neither campaign for the ticket nor repudiate it, a tactic that disgusted NSRP leaders.

In March 1964, the party met in convention at Louisville, Kentucky—while CORE pickets walked outside the hotel—and picked two candidates closer to the NSRP cause for the forthcoming presidential election. For the presidency, it offers John Kasper, of Nashville, Tennessee—organizer of the Seaboard White Citizens Councils—who has served three prison sentences for racist activity (two federal terms for interfering with federal court orders, and a term in Nashville for inciting a riot). The party's vice presidential nominee is Jesse B. Stoner, former Imperial Wizard of the Christian Knights of the Ku Klux Klan and presently the NSRP's legal counselor.

NSRP candidates are already on the ballot in Kentucky and Arkansas, and the party is attempting to get on the ballot in other states—with the notable exception of Alabama. The exception of Alabama results from the NSRP's great admiration for Governor George C. Wallace, their favorite among Southern politicians. The party worked for the slate of unpledged electors, a scheme successfully used by Wallace to win in Alabama. Party Information Director Fields says the NSRP is indebted to Wallace for speeches he made protesting the arrest of its members in Birmingham last September.

In June 1963, the NSRP outdid all its previous anti-Semitic outbursts by reprinting the May 1934 issue of Julius Streicher's *Der Stürmer.* This was Streicher's ghastly "Ritual Murder" issue. The reprint—in German except for a few explanatory captions and an advertisement—shows drawings of Jewish elders sucking blood through straws from the body of a dead gentile child, and rabbis catching blood flowing from wounds inflicted upon gentile women. Most of this material comes from medieval writings reflecting the insane superstition of the dark ages, and was widely circulated by Streicher. Arnold Leese's book, *Jewish Ritual Murder,* published and distributed by the NSRP, contains all of this material in English.

The reprint of this *Der Stürmer* issue was a bonus to go with the June *Thunderbolt* and was offered, the editor said, "In memory of Julius Streicher, who was murdered to appease the Jews." An English caption under Streicher's Nazi-uniformed portrait said, in part: "Let this new edition of his most famous issue be a living monument to his courage and fortitude in exposing the Jew Menace, even though it cost him his life."

The author of this warm salute to a Nazi war criminal is Dr. Edward R. Fields, a chiropractor, who has been active in anti-Semitic groups since he was fourteen years old. He was associated with the Columbians, an avowedly neo-Nazi group in Atlanta, where he grew up. Fields says he is "dedicated to the task of saving America and the White Race and the preservation of the pure blood of our forefathers." As information director of the party, he is responsible for the day-to-day direction of most party activities and edits the monthly paper.

Reprints from other anti-Semitic publications such as Conde McGinley's *Common Sense* and Gerald L.K. Smith's *The Cross and the Flag* fill many pages of *The Thunderbolt.* The party organ also reprints stories of murder and rape and other crimes if the accused are Negroes or persons thought to be Jewish. It has inaugurated a new series recently featuring "The Jew of the Month"—usually a thief, racketeer, or murderer.

One article, dreamed up by Fields himself and published in October 1963, charges that the Federal Bureau of Investigation is part of the "Communist-Jewish conspiracy." Unlike other right-wing groups which lavish praise on FBI Director J. Edgar Hoover—even to the extent of suggesting he run for President—the NSRP finds nothing to admire about him. After FBI agents questioned party members about the bombing of the 16th Street Baptist Church in Birmingham, Fields retaliated by issuing a special bulletin calling the FBI "a secret police" and gave "fourteen instances of FBI intimidation." Hoover was called a "violent race-mixer," and the bulletin asked: "With all of J. Edgar Hoover's mixed and mongrel friends, we would like to ask Hoover this question:'J. Edgar Hoover, with all your kinky hair, flat nose, bulgy eyes, etc., just what is your race?'" Hoover was warned that "his days in office were numbered."

While the John Birch Society campaigns to force the impeachment of Chief Justice Earl Warren, the NSRP finds this approach too mild. Fields and the NSRP demand that the chief justice and the eight associate justices be put to death. *The Thunderbolt* said: "The number-one plan of Communist subversion is to destroy the Whiteman through Mongrelization with the Blackman. Federal law provides for the death penalty for all who give 'aid and comfort to America's enemies.' It is our position that the present members of the Supreme Court are guilty of treason and should be thusly tried and given the Ultimate Penalty."

Throughout the trial of Adolph Eichmann in Israel, *The Thunderbolt* attempted to raise money for something called the Eichmann Trial Facts Committee. The NSRP insisted that stories of Nazi atrocities and the deaths of millions of Jews were "a giant propaganda hoax" but, *The Thunderbolt* said, "If spies, traitors, and Communists were executed in Germany during the war—and they turned out for the most part to be Jews—so what? Are we going to crawl in the dirt in the name of Jewry, and beg the Jews to forgive the White Race because a Whiteman once meted out Justice to the Jews? I say, 'No, a thousand times no!' We are going to fight these greedy scheming Jews, who seek to destroy our race, nation, and faith and everything we hold dear. Whatever the final solution to the Jewish problem turns out to be, it will be the Jew who brings it on himself."

The party's solution—when it takes power—is to deport the Jews to Madagascar and "to confiscate the wealth of Jews for the benefit of the

American people." A point system would be established for NSRP patriots who have labored to rid America of all Jewish influence. The United Nations, communism, and race mixing are all cited as being Jewish-inspired. A patriot can gain points by fighting these forces. All of this is set out in the April 1963 issue of *The Thunderbolt*, which declares: " . . . Money, gold, businesses, and property that the Jews unrighteously possess will legally be taken away by the United States government and given to us. The Jews have too much money, but someday it will be ours."

While the NSRP's main themes are anti-Jewish, the party is also anti-Negro, anti-Oriental, anti-Mexican, and opposed to immigration from any place but Northern or "Nordic" Europe. The Negro is usually described in NSRP literature as a stupid, docile, ape-like creature that becomes a wild animal when excited by the Jews, who are the force behind civil rights demands. A recent issue of *The Thunderbolt* carries a chart giving the characteristics of Negroes and apes, and the conclusion is that Negroes and apes are the same. "The Negro is still in the ape stage," the writer says, "and is actually a higher form of gorilla. God did not wish for the White race to mix with these animals." Various "scientific" studies are cited to support these and similar assertions. One cited study, financed by the State of Alabama and recently released by Governor Wallace, claims the Negro race is 200,000 years behind the white race in the process of evolution.

One of the significant factors in the growth of the NSRP has been its ability to get right-wing and other anti-Semitic groups to join with it in forming a larger party, and "to get on the NSRP bandwagon and ride to victory in 1968." It has absorbed the United White Party, the Conservative Party of America, another States Rights Party, the Constitution Party of Iowa, and several other small groups, while attracting individuals from various White Citizens Council and Klan groups.

The NSRP longs to become a true mass movement, directed by its present "true believers." Although critical of the Klan as faint-hearted, its doctrines resemble those that led to the Klan's growth in the 1920s. It officially denies the militant anti-Catholicism of the Klan, but statements printed in *The Thunderbolt* about the late Pope John would infuriate most Catholics. *The Thunderbolt* said that "conservative Catholics were shocked by Pope John's appeasement of Communists," and called the deleting of the term "perfidious Jews" from Catholic prayers a "disturbing trend." It linked the late pontiff's name with that of Khrushchev and communist Gus Hall and added, "The best we can say for the man is that he does not know what he is doing."

The NSRP is following trails blazed by the Klan, which at its peak in the '20s had four million members. It boasted 500,000 Klansmen in Indiana, 450,000 in Ohio, 200,000 in New York, another 200,000 in California, and controlled politics in several midwestern states, including Indiana and Kansas. The NSRP has adopted the tactics of the Klan in suiting its appeal to the region—it is anti-Oriental on the West Coast, anti-Mexican in the Southwest, wants the Indians kept on reservations, is anti-Negro in the South, and anti-immigrant in areas where immigration is made to seem like a threat to the job security of residents.

The NSRP membership falls into three main groups:

> One–the controlling circle of leaders, made up of anti-Semites, former Ku Klux Klansmen, and the leaders of groups absorbed by the NSRP.
>
> Two–militant segregationists who have been attracted to the party because of the partial failure of white resistance efforts to stem desegregation.
>
> Three–youthful adherents who are attracted by uniforms, the conspiratorial nature of the party, and its militant activist approach. Fields's chief lieutenants in Birmingham are in their teens or early twenties. The California leaders of the NSRP are of college age.

That the Jew is responsible for every misfortune and event that has afflicted mankind is repeated endlessly in party publications and speeches. President Kennedy was attacked in 1963 issues of *The Thunderbolt* as a race-mixer and tool of the Communist-Jewish conspiracy. The January 1964 issue headlined a story: "Jews INVOLVED IN ASSASSINATION?" This issue featured an "exclusive" interview with Admiral John G. Crommelin, the NSRP's one-time vice-presidential nominee, who is not actually a member of the party but who acts as a kind of father-confessor and den mother to the Birmingham group. According to *The Thunderbolt*, Crommelin believes that Kennedy was assassinated by the Communist-Jewish conspiracy. Why? Crommelin is reported as explaining that

Kennedy had become a political liability to the Jews because of a tremendous wave of unpopularity.

The NSRP came into Birmingham heralding itself as advancing "The Whiteman's Viewpoint." Much of the Birmingham community, so long acclimated to the doctrines of white supremacy, accepted these particular "outsiders" who were fighting the desegregation of Birmingham schools ordered by federal courts. Birmingham leaders have of course bewailed and bemoaned the presence of other "outsiders," saying they were in the city to foment trouble and discord among Negroes. "Outsiders" for white Birmingham means persons like Atlanta resident Dr. Martin Luther King, Jr. and his aides.

Only one of the twelve to fifteen active leaders in the NSRP in Birmingham is a bona fide resident of the city. Those Birmingham leaders who recognized the NSRP movement as anti-Semitic were afraid to raise a voice against the group for fear of being labeled "Nigger lover," still a potent epithet in Alabama. A "Nigger lover" in Birmingham is the recipient of harassing telephone calls, threats of all kinds, and faces possible job loss and other economic reprisals. If it had not been for the NSRP and kindred forces, and the resistance leadership headed by Governor Wallace, school desegregation in the city could have been accomplished in relative peace.

The immediate danger of the party lies in its proven ability to infiltrate other groups and use to its advantage the fears of a community in racial crisis. When some parents with children at high schools affected by Birmingham desegregation called meetings to encourage boycotts of the schools and the formation of private schools, the NSRP infiltrated the gatherings and called additional meetings where parents and students were regaled by party speakers. One group of parents with children in West End High School felt forced to buy radio time to advertise that a meeting called by the NSRP was not a legitimate meeting of the West End parents group.

It should be noted that the party has no abiding interest in the issues of any crisis. The future of the party is its primary concern, and exploiting racial problems is only one of its chosen roads to mass growth. With the advance of desegregation and increased civil rights activity of all kinds, dozens of segregationist groups have emerged in opposition. People who hate or fear Negroes have joined these groups. Of all the groups formed, the NSRP is the most virulent in the fostering of hate. Some of the top leaders of the party remain in the national headquarters at Birmingham, while other state and local leaders from various parts of the country come there to visit Fields and his aides. They return home, inspired by the success of the NSRP in Birmingham, to spread their racist gospel among the ignorant and the fear-ridden, wherever they may be.

What happened and is happening in Birmingham is not so singular that it cannot happen elsewhere, for Birmingham is merely an exaggeration of every city with a real or even an imagined racial problem. Whether the six-year-old National States Rights Party grows or declines to the point where even a Wallace disavows it will be decided by the manner in which communities throughout the nation face advancing desegregation.

Right now, the Negro "problem" is the key to party expansion. "We get a lot of help from the Niggers," says David Stanley, a Canadian youth at Birmingham headquarters. "They help us bring attention to the damned Jews who are behind it all."

There it is. In spite of the party's exploitation of the civil rights problem, the Jews rank first in its priority of hatreds; then the Negroes, second; other minorities, third; the FBI; the United Nations; even the Birch Society. Crackpots, maybe, but not harmless crackpots as long as they can help escalate hate into violence.

[According to Wikipedia, accessed December 2, 2015: "The party's influence declined in the 1970s, as chief ideologue Fields began to devote more of his energies to the Ku Klux Klan. As a result, in April 1976 U.S. Attorney General Edward H. Levi concluded an FBI investigation into the group, after it was decided that they posed no threat. In the 1980s, the NSRP began its terminal decline when Stoner was convicted for a bombing in 1980. Without his leadership, the party descended into factionalism, and in August 1983 Fields was expelled for spending too much time in the KKK. Without its two central figures the NSRP fell apart, and by 1987 it had ceased to exist altogether."]

# Alabama Observations

11–21–94

Dear Joey:

Thanks for the article on [Elizabeth H.] Cobbs/ [Petric J.] Smith. That family member who told on Dynamite Bob Chambliss was a niece/ nephew who got her boobs and other female equipment removed, took testosterone, and grew a beard. Very Alabama, Joey. Truth is always weird; no one could put a twist that odd into fiction. This I know for certain: Cobbs/Smith has courage and a good heart.

Dynamite Bob was himself contradictory: devoted and dangerous, threatening and affectionate, a gentle group-centered accidentally-but-on-purpose killer of children.

I remember that bloody day in detail, trying to get close enough to gather information for a stringer story, trying to stay out of pictures as I was certain to be fired if the Ensley steelworkers learned what I was

---

Joe Wilson wrote: "This is a letter to Joey Brackner, then Alabama state folklorist. Joey had sent me a news clip about a relative of Robert Chambliss, the Birmingham bomber who placed the drip-bucket bomb under the 16th Street Baptist Church in 1963. I wrote about that for *The Progressive* in June of 1964."

doing. My stuff was published as by "Joseph Wilson," but neither the National States Rights Party, Kluxers, or Stephenson ever really put it all together. The FBI did.

I interviewed the Birmingham agent in charge in early 1964, and he knew of my *Progressive* tie. He didn't care for it. *The Progressive* had been critical of J. Edgar, the first publication to take a shot at that holy man—or was he really a woman? The rumor that he was a secret cross-dresser who spent a part of every evening attached to Clyde Tolson still follows him. As I said, weird.

The old values pass, the new becomes antique, and the old holy is subjected to sudden rigorous doubt. All those splinters of the true cross—that cured goiter, gave visions, and made thousands tremble on holy days—were eventually inherited by louts who used them as toothpicks. There's always the possibility that when you put out your tongue to receive the wafer, a passing pigeon will take a shot at it. Not a passenger pigeon, Joey. They've already passed.

And for your good deed in sending that fascinating story, you receive in return this fountain of pish-posh.

I'm still getting my Birmingham years FBI file through Freedom of Information. It is a tedious and slow business. All that I have learned so far is that "a multiple page file exists."

All the best,
Joe

In December 2015, Carolyn Fuller read this letter and wrote:

> That was a hard fall. I knew one of the girls who was blown up in the 16th Street Baptist Church bombing. I was a sophomore at Ramsay High School. My mom was one of the parents who brought a civil suit against [Alabama Governor George C.] Wallace for closing the schools.
>
> I was the only person in the school who, at lunch in the school cafeteria, would sit with Richard Walker, the young black student. I am sure I made a great lunchtime companion. I felt so weak, helpless, and useless. But that didn't stop a former acquaintance from waiting for me to exit the school so he could beat me up. I knew him from the Unitarian Church. His family had left the Church because of the Church's decision to embrace the Civil Rights Movement. Fortunately, a friend warned me and I exited from a different door.

Another afternoon that fall, I was late getting home from school because I had my regularly scheduled Junior Achievement program. But my mom had forgotten that, and she had received a phone call that I would be arriving home that evening in ten pieces. She was a basket case by the time I got home.

There were many nights that fall that I slept under the dining room table with a pillow on top of me to protect against the possibility of flying glass. We got multiple threatening phone calls every day. We counted getting them every thirteen minutes one day. And then it was all topped off by my high school teacher, leading the class in applause when JFK was assassinated in November.

And then there was Joe, fighting those bastards in the most creative and maybe not precisely legal ways. He was my beacon!

# FOLKLORE AND FOLK FESTIVALS

# The Talmadge Visit

Archie Green was a master in bringing together the like-minded. He had a task for everyone and urged on the unlikely coalition of academicians, labor activists, record collectors, and arts presenters who had an inkling of what amounted to folk arts. These were mainly very progressive folks, and the list of sponsors of our bills revealed those inclinations without anything being said.

Yet it was a time when signs of major social adjustments in the nation were arriving almost daily. Ten years had passed since Lyndon Johnson had intoned Guy Carawan's loaded musical phrase "We shall overcome" into a microphone with the nation listening, signaling a huge readjustment in the Democratic Party. The nation does not instantly do anything, but a process began, and it was having huge effect. Arch-segregationist Senator Strom Thurmond had just hired a black staffer, and the entire

---

Undated and presumably unpublished. Joe's manuscript ended in mid-sentence, so it may have been unfinished. In the early 1970s, Joe and folklorist Archie Green (1917–2009) lobbied Congress to pass the American Folklife Preservation Act (P.L. 94-201), which led to the creation of the American Folklife Center within the Library of Congress.

South knew without anything being said that a giant political Rubicon had been crossed.

I was fresh from Dixie and suggested to Archie that we needed more Deep South support. He gave me a bemused Archie look, saying, in effect, "You'll need to drive."

But he went with me to see Senator Herman Talmadge of Georgia. I knew some of the Talmadge staff from work for the Atlanta University group of colleges, realizing that some were eager to improve the Talmadge reputation of being the most unreconstructed of the wool-hat generation.

Talmadge prided himself on seeing any citizen of Georgia who entered his office. His election pledge to do that was from many years earlier, before the interstates and hourly flights from Atlanta brought a daily flood of favor-seeking Georgians to Gotham-by-the-Potomac. So he tended to see visitors for twenty seconds or less. Even so, there was a line when we arrived.

A photograph on the wall, near the end of the line where the senator stood glad-handing, grabbed my attention. It showed Governor Eugene Talmadge, father of the senator, standing in the back of a Model T truck, campaigning in a small town in the 1930s, wearing his trademark suspenders and gesturing to heaven. I was still engrossed in telling Archie about it when our time came.

"That's my father," Talmadge said, to get our attention. "Yessir," I responded, tapping the figure of a man with a fiddle case under his arm, "and that is Fiddlin' John Carson; I think he may have just played 'Georgia's Three Dollar Tag.'"

Carson was the first of the successful old-time recording pioneers of the 1920s, and his complaint that there was no use in "putting a thirty-dollar tag on a ten-dollar car"—put to a Bluebird 78 rpm disc—had helped Eugene Talmadge win the governorship. The Atlanta street fiddler and Cabbagetown resident had been a fixture of Talmadge family campaigning for two generations.

I wish you could have been there to see the smile on the face of Herman Talmadge. "Good Lord, Son, you know about that? Could you help me get a copy of that old recording?"

I told him it would be no problem, but I'd need a few days. "Then you can do something the president of the University of Georgia could not do," he said. "I need it for my father's papers." I assured him I thought I could locate a copy, and after brief chit-chat Archie and I moved on to tell staff what we needed from the senator.

A couple of weeks later Archie and I were again in the senator's visitor line, and I handed him a good condition copy of Fiddlin' John's recording of the old campaign song about the cost of a tag for a chugging flivver on the dusty roads of Georgia in the days of yore. Collector Frank Mare had helped me find it by canvassing other country music collectors. Talmadge looked carefully at it, then gently placed it on his desk and led Archie and me to where his chief of staff worked.

"These boys have a good bill we are co-sponsoring," he said. "Talk to them and see if they need other senators as sponsors. We want to help these boys."

There were other memorable moments when our cause was advanced, but here—in an instant—a powerful advocate was recruited. Yet it was a moment steeped in personal conflict for Archie. Talmadge represented much that Archie Green despised, and it was not easy for the ship's carpenter from San Francisco to make common cause with him. Archie was a justice-seeker, the dutiful son of a father who had fled the wrath of a czar. To seek equality in league with a politician from a family steeped in racism had not been on his agenda.

I tried to get Archie to understand the "big tent" concept of large-party politics. When I finished my spiel, Archie asked that I apply these humane American rules to the Romanov family and czarist Russia.

"First, Archie, you gotta understand that no dictator is going to understand a group of kids who are bent on croaking his ass."

His laughter filled the hall, and he begged, "Let me get out of here before I have to masticate number two."

Other experiences were equally hard: "progressive" members of Congress who would not help, and—even worse—some who promised support and tendered none.

Politics is practical work, a dance with the angels of mercy but also with the devil.

# Joe Wilson at the Helm of the NCTA

*Eugenia Snyder*

With the title of executive director of the National Council for the Traditional Arts (NCTA) and a work address on prestigious Connecticut Avenue in Washington, D.C., you might expect Joe Wilson to be an Ivy League graduate with the kind of financial well-being which permits members of certain families to dabble in the arts without the weighty concerns of home mortgage payments and such. At the very least, you might expect Joe Wilson to be the tweedy professorial type, the kind of man who has put traditional (in the sense of "common") concerns aside to devote his life to the study of an academic interest. But Joe Wilson is neither.

With an intoxicating Tennessee accent and a demeanor so relaxed that it belies the level of his passion for and involvement in his work, Joe Wilson is a man through whose veins flows the blood of the mountains, of Appalachia, of country life as it was and as he wishes it could still be. He dons not Brooks Brothers suits, khaki slacks, nor Ralph Lauren shirts, but brand X jeans, Hawaiian shirts, western boots, and, when necessary,

---

Excerpted from "Joe Wilson: A Bluegrasser at the Helm of the NCTA," *Bluegrass Unlimited*, April 1986.

a sport coat and slacks. He works not in a modern office with a spacious executive desk and diplomas and tasteful pictures hung in neat rows on the walls, but in a rather dingy, cluttered room where Indian corn husk masks peer down with vacant expressions from the walls and a blue and orange bumper sticker warns: "Pass at your own risk—I chew tobacco."

Joe's charm and his ability to mingle with equal ease among Washington politicians, wealthy socialites, and backwoods artisans come not from a formal education and advantaged upbringing, but from his innate intelligence, an unparalleled devotion to the truly ethnic, and years of self-application. His wit and his sense of humor pave his way into people's hearts and, when the occasion calls for it, into their pocketbooks and bank accounts as well.

Though it is based in Washington and possesses an official sounding title, the NCTA is not an entity of the federal government. It is a private, nonprofit organization which receives funds from government agencies such as the National Endowment for the Arts and the National Endowment for the Humanities, from state arts councils, and from a large number of private sources. With a two-room office and a salaried staff of four, the NCTA is not a large organization, but it is an important one. Under Joe's direction, the NCTA is responsible for exploring, defining, and presenting America's traditional arts—arts which range from decoy carving, chair-making, and weaving to Creole Zydeco music, Yiddish theater, Swedish American music, Native American dance, and bluegrass.

Surrounded by books, records, audiotapes, videotapes, slides, sound equipment, and the miscellaneous debris of NCTA projects, Joe, his staff, and scores of volunteer members of the NCTA engage in a myriad of arts-related activities. They produce the National Folk Festival (an annual tradition initiated in 1934) and advise and assist state and local arts councils in producing folk festivals and promoting the traditional arts. They organize tours of American (and sometimes foreign) artists, craftsmen, and musicians—both in this country and abroad—and assist in the production of radio and television shows. They produce movies, travel, research, record, and photograph. "Sometimes I think we work on too many things—we get stretched real thin," Joe said, "but we usually pull things off one way or the other."

As an individual, Joe Wilson also serves as a one-man clearinghouse of information on the arts. Blessed with an insatiable appetite for information, an unrelenting intellectual curiosity, and nearly total recall, he is able to talk at length on history, the arts, and a host of other subjects. He is uniquely qualified for his position at the NCTA, and his talents and resources are tapped by folks from all around. He works well beyond the usual 9:00 to 5:00, Monday through Friday, because, as he confessed, he has "a hard time saying no."

When the NCTA Board of Trustees began looking for a new executive director in 1976, Joe was an obvious choice. Though he was, by then, a vice president of Oram Group in New York City, he was only too happy to accept a "humongous cut in pay" to work full-time at what had been a lifelong interest. He left Madison Avenue and moved to Washington.

Over the years, Joe may have strayed away from Appalachia and a career in country music, but he never left them far behind. While working for the Oram Group, he found time to research, support, and promote traditional country music. He read whatever was written about the music and musicians, he returned home to Tennessee and revived the Mountain City Fiddlers' Convention, and he befriended others in the New York area who were interested in helping country music not only survive, but prosper. He planned tours for musicians and organized concerts in New York featuring Bill Monroe, Ted Lundy, Bob Paisley, Kyle Creed, Tommy Jarrell, and other great Southern musicians.

Joe believes that the NCTA's role is to bring the traditional arts to people—to increase the extent to which they are recognized, understood, and appreciated. Under his leadership, the NCTA's goal has been one of propagation, not preservation. "Things are preserved as long as people have good ears and want to preserve them," he said. "This place is stuffed with slides and tapes, and we do our best to keep a record of what we do, because we think it will be important to somebody sometime . . . or at least part of it will. But I'm not sure you can preserve anything by putting it in a glass case.

"Preservation turns an item into an artifact," he continued. "A song lives as long as you and I are singing it, or maybe even thinking about it, or planning to sing it again. If we don't do that, it dies and becomes an item on a collector's shelf. I'm ready to agree that it still has value, but I swear I don't believe it has as much value. The things that live in your heart and in your head are the things that are truly important."

And Joe Wilson's future? Well, he's happy right where he is, doing just what he's doing. His "work" could only be improved by adding more dollars to the NCTA's coffer, more people to the NCTA's payroll, and more hours to each day. But even without additional dollars, staff members, and hours Joe is likely to thrive at the NCTA. "I know I'll never die of boredom!" he said.

# Beginnings of the National Folk Festival

The use of the term "folk festival" appears to be of relatively recent vintage in the United States. In 1892, it was used in advertising literature printed by Hampton Institute, Virginia, to describe the performances of musicians traveling with the Hampton Jubilee Singers. In the early 1900s, it was used by the Henry Street Settlement House in New York City and by Hull House in Chicago to describe the performances of recent immigrants at settlement house events.

In 1928, Bascom Lamar Lunsford inaugurated his Mountain Dance and Folk Festival in Asheville, North Carolina. This was a celebration of Southern Appalachian music and dance, and resembled the large fiddlers' conventions then being held in Atlanta, Georgia; Mountain City, Tennessee; and elsewhere in the South. His festival differed from the older fiddlers' conventions in that he used the self-conscious term "folk festival." The use of this term says much about Lunsford's intent, particu-

---

Adapted from the program book for the 50th National Folk Festival, 1988, Lowell, Massachusetts, National Council for the Traditional Arts, and chapter one of *Folk Festivals: A Handbook for Organization and Management*, by Joe Wilson and Lee Udall, copyright 1982 by the University of Tennessee Press: Knoxville.

larly his concern that a larger public know and respect mountain music and dance. Lunsford's festival became an annual event.

The first National Folk Festival was held April 29 to May 2, 1934, in St. Louis, Missouri. It was the first folk festival to present the cultural expressions of several ethnic and regional groups on the same stage, and it was the first to utilize the skills of persons trained in folklore and related disciplines.

Two persons were largely responsible for the creation of this event. The idea originated with Sarah Gertrude Knott. In November 1933, she chartered the National Folk Festival and she served as its director. Knott adopted Lunsford's use of the term "folk festival," but her concept differed significantly; her purpose was to present the diversity and richness of American folk culture to audiences unfamiliar with this material. Major M.J. Pickering was business manager and persuaded a group of St. Louis businessmen to serve as guarantors for the $13,000 necessary to mount the festival.

Neither knew much about folk arts, but Knott and Pickering both had experience in creating large-scale performing events. Knott had produced theatrical extravaganzas in North Carolina and St. Louis, and had directed a citywide performance series funded by the Federal Emergency Relief Act, as St. Louis inched its way out of the depths of the Great Depression.

Pickering was a lawyer who had earned his degree in night school. His military rank was earned in a U.S. Army Air Service squadron during World War I. The general manager of the St. Louis Coliseum when he became interested in the National, Pickering had been involved in bookings and management for major arenas since starting this part of his career a dozen years earlier at Yankee Stadium.

Both were in their middle years. Miss Knott was thirty-nine. Major Pickering was fifty-four. He would remain with the festival for eighteen years, until 1951. Miss Knott gave up direction of the festival in 1970 and retired to Kentucky, but she never really left it. The dancers and the musicians and the crowds who came to cheer them were her life, and she continued to be obsessed with performance and organizational plans until her death in 1984 at the age of eighty-nine.

Folklorists who know their forebears will find the festival Miss Knott and Major Pickering created in 1934 very interesting. Cultural specialists—such as folklorists, ethnomusicologists, and historians—brought to the festival both their skills and the great regional and ethnic artists they had found. Many of the pioneers of workaday folklore helped to create this first multi-ethnic folk festival. And with them was one of the most entertaining of the nation's perpetrators of folkloric fiction, then engaged in her biggest scam.

Miss Knott spent more than a year writing, visiting and requesting the cooperation of these specialists, and Major Pickering's funding efforts made it possible for them to participate. Some of the most notable of the contributors to the early festival were:

O.B. JACOBSON, director of the School of Art, University of Oklahoma, who brought a group of Kiowa and Comanche Indian singers and dancers. Kiowa groups continued to come to the National for the next fifteen years, and Jacobson became a member of the board.

HELEN HARTNESS FLANDERS, director of the Archive of Vermont Folk Songs, who presented Elmer George, a fine ballad singer from East Calais, Vermont.

GEORGE PULLEN JACKSON, a professor in the English Department at Vanderbilt University and author of *White Spirituals in the Southern Uplands*, who presented and participated in the singing of The Old Harp Singers, users of the four-shape-note nineteenth century hymnal, *The Sacred Harp*. He was involved in subsequent festivals.

ARTHUR L. CAMPA, director of research at the University of New Mexico, who brought Spanish-speaking actors and singers to the festival. The actors performed the New Mexico village drama, *Los Pastores* (The Shepherds), an anonymous religious play of considerable antiquity. Campa was to remain involved with the National for forty-one years, serving on the board and as president of the board.

ZORA NEALE HURSTON, then teaching at Bethune-Cookman College and hating every hour of it, who brought singers, dancers, and bluesmen from Eatonville and Daytona Beach, Florida. The irrepressible Miss Hurston heard that others would be doing plays, so she brought one (*De Fiery Chariot—Dramatized Folk-tale*), creating a good part for herself and acting in it along with two members of her troupe.

The Eatonville group performed blues and railroad work songs with spiking and track-lining rhythms and what was called an "African Survival Ritual—survived from African background but with American modifications." They did a fire dance that Zora Neale called ". . . . a sort of creation expression, a new birth of life. When new leaves appear on a certain tree, the dances begin." Was Zora Neale pulling the chain of staid St. Louis and her fellow folklorists? She was.

Like all the other folklorists, Miss Hurston came knowing "there's no money in it." She became a member of the advisory board and returned with her Eatonville friends five years later when the festival came to Washington's Constitution Hall. That year (1938) she shared the National's stage with W.C. Handy, father of the blues form she so dearly loved.

Other scholar-collectors who came to St. Louis in 1934 included:

J. FRANK DOBIE, professor at the University of Texas and president of the Texas Folklore Society, who was a participant in the academic conclave that was held in conjunction with the festival. He became a friend and long-term advisor of the festival.

LEO B. REAGAN, a Connecticut collector of maritime lore, who brought a group of retired before-the-mast sailors from the Sailor's Snug Harbor retirement home at Staten Island, New York, to sing sea chanteys.

VANCE RANDOLPH, author and self-taught Ozark folklorist, who met and advised Miss Knott during her trips to the Ozarks while she was planning the festival. He participated in the academic conclave and joined the advisory board.

CECILIA BERRY, a collector from Vincennes, Indiana, who directed a group of French descendants from that town in singing French folk songs traditional to Indiana. Another group of Mississippi Valley French, from Saint Genevieve, Missouri, performed a staged version of the Mississippi Valley mumming custom, *La Guignolee*.

MAY KENNEDY MCCORD, Missouri Ozarks singer, collector, and newspaper columnist, who assisted Miss Knott in securing an excellent contingent of Ozark participants. They became lifelong friends.

FREDERICK KOCH, director of the Carolina Playmakers and Kenan Professor at the University of North Carolina, who brought his troupe to perform three plays with "folk" themes (Miss Knott included "folk" plays in the first three Nationals, but they did not stay in the folk festival mix after that). Professor Koch was Miss Knott's mentor and had been her employer in North Carolina. He was the first president of the National Folk Festival Association, the nonprofit association that would evolve into the National Council for the Traditional Arts.

ROMAINE LOWDERMILK and JACK WIDMER of the Soda Springs Ranch at Rimrock, Arizona, old-time cowboys who performed cowboy songs and discussed them in the academic conclave.

CONSTANCE ROURKE, a collector and folklorist living in Grand Rapids, Michigan, who brought the first contingent of lumberjacks to this festival. They fiddled, danced jigs and clogs, and sang bunkhouse songs. Lumberjacks were to become a tradition at the National; a Wisconsin group had the longest tenure, performing regularly for over twenty years.

BASCOM LAMAR LUNSFORD, musician and avid collector of Appalachian materials, who brought singers, dancers, and instrumentalists to this festival from western North Carolina. A favorite was the old-time fiddler Pender Rector. The director of an Asheville festival sponsored by the Chamber of Commerce that specialized in Appalachian materials, Lunsford had helped Miss Knott choose participants for the National at his 1933 event. He joined the board and became a warm friend and regular participant.

JEAN BELL THOMAS, founder of the American Folk Song Festival at Ashland, Kentucky, who brought "Jilson Setters, 'The Singing Fiddler' of Lost Hope Hollow, Kentucky" to the festival. A note in the program book says, "Two years ago, Miss Thomas took Jilson Setters to London, England to participate in the English Folk Festival, held in Albert Hall. 'The Singing Fiddler' took back to England the language and the balladry of the Elizabethan days, which his family had brought to this country several hundred years ago."

Behind this romantic stereotyping is a fiction. Jilson Setters never existed. Miss Thomas created "The Singing Fiddler" from her imagination. She is said to have been inspired by Blind Ed Haley, a Kentucky street and courthouse square fiddler of amazing ability. She thought that the press would like Haley better if he pretended to be more country than he was. So she decided that he should wear homespun, carry an oak split egg basket, and speak a more rustic English. His name would be rusticated to a more mountain-sounding one. He would become Jilson Setters.

A Kentucky court reporter in her youth, Miss Thomas had moved to Greenwich Village, where she gained some understanding of what rural stereotypes were most appealing to the urban cognoscenti. She lived in Hollywood and had worked on the original *The Ten Commandments* film. She believed in contracts, publicity, and context. Back in Kentucky, she began calling herself "The Traipsin' Woman" and organized her festival in 1930. The Jilson Setters idea allowed her to put all her skills to work. She began writing a book, *The Singing Fiddler of Lost Hope Hollow*, and found a major publisher.

There was one problem. Blind Ed Haley would have no part in such a humbug—but Miss Thomas was too involved with her story to let a small detail deter her. She found another blind Appalachian fiddler to play the role of the secluded fiddler. He was J.W. Day, who had earlier made 78 rpm commercial recordings for Victor.

The book was popular and the New York press very receptive. In England, it is said that Day/Setters performed for, among others, the chinless wonder who would become the short-lived King of England and the long-lived Duke of Windsor. There's a rumor that Miss Thomas made more money from her book than Jilson did from his fiddling. There is, sadly, no record of how Miss Thomas fared in the festival's academic session when she read a paper about Jilson's exploits to such plainspoken folklorists as Vance Randolph and George Pullen Jackson.

Other than program books and news clippings, records of the first festival are scant. Miss Knott figured prominently in the press reviews and editorials that greeted the first festival. These seem to have been uniformly laudatory. Many of the artists and folklorists who participated came to later festivals, a good indication of satisfaction. But there would not be another National in St. Louis for twelve years. This was because of financing.

The guarantors who put up the $13,000 were just that—guarantors. The festival was intended to be self-supporting through box office sales. Box office fell "several thousand" short and the guarantors took a bath. These were years when a new car could be had for six or seven hundred dollars, and $20-a-week jobs were cherished. Miss Knott recalled that the same guarantors usually underwrote an annual deficit for the Municipal Opera, but were unwilling to do this for the folk festival.

There were no further options in St. Louis, but other cities had noted the considerable publicity the festival received and expressed interest.

Miss Knott and Major Pickering had to decide what to do with their lives—back to the old grind or on to another folk festival in another city?

The second National Folk Festival was held May 14 to 18, 1935, in Chattanooga, Tennessee, and was remarkably like the first one. Many artists who had been in St. Louis repeated. The festival was especially rich in central South religious and string band music. Folklorist George Korson brought a contingent of anthracite coal miners from eastern Pennsylvania; he became a member of the National's board and an organizer of Pennsylvania festivals.

But there were major differences in scale when the third National was held in Dallas in June 1936. This festival was part of the exposition celebrating the Texas centennial, and it was bigger—six stages instead of one or two, and eight days rather than five. A half-century later, portions of it seem wonderfully exotic. For example, the "Tale-Telling" sessions with a Major Black telling about "Ranger Days," slave stories by former slaves, Billy The Kid stories from a man who knew him, stories about Indian fights by people who were in them, and Comanches telling their side of the fight stories.

It was the first folk festival to have a Louisiana Cajun band, and it had four. These were S.S. Broussard's Acadian Band from Lake Arthur; the Evangeline Band from St. Martinsville, led by Wade Bernard; Ardus Broussard's Acadian Band from Rayne; and the Hackberry Band from Rayne.

There was a huge quilt and coverlet show, and eighty-four-year-old Mrs. Cinderella Kinnaird of Willow Spring, Missouri, demonstrated weaving. Two hundred residents of Anson, Texas, reenacted their famous *Cowboy's Christmas Ball*, and Mr. Staples of Dixfield, Maine, came to sing ballads wearing his wedding suit of 1878.

Among the nineteen Texas fiddle bands were the East Texas Serenaders and Albert L. Steeley's Fiddling Three (earlier, The Red Headed Fiddlers). There were Sacred Harp singers from Georgia and Texas. There were black shape-note singers and Cherokee shape-note singers who rendered camp meeting hymns in Cherokee. There were chanteymen from Galveston to join with those from Snug Harbor and even an old trail drivers' reunion. There was work lore and crafts of many kinds. Folklorist Ben A. Botkin came to his first National and was to remain associated with it for the rest of his life as a board member or president.

In subsequent years, other folklorists and collectors were associated with Miss Knott in producing National Folk Festivals in seventeen cities. Many of these festivals were sponsored by daily newspapers, such as the *St. Louis Globe-Democrat*, the *New York Post*, the *Milwaukee Journal*, the *Philadelphia Inquirer*, and the *Washington Post*.

Major Pickering made vital contributions to the development of the modern folklife festival. He left in 1951, before the surge of interest in the 1960s. But even a cursory analysis of the early festivals shows that he kept the enterprise on track. Miss Knott had the initial idea and avidly pursued new programming concepts and options. She gave the interviews and served as emcee at the festival. Pickering handled the organizational matters. His letters reveal a man of good intellect and sharp wit, a friend of the artists. He sought the assistance of friends in the foreign service in bringing folk groups from other nations to the festival. Pickering later organized some festivals on his own; these included the Golden Gate International Exposition in San Francisco in 1939 and the festival that accompanied the opening of the United Nations in 1946.

The prewar National Folk Festivals reached their zenith in Washington, D.C., during 1938–41 with Agnes Meyer, wife of the publisher of the *Washington Post*, as chairman of the events. The sponsoring organization—the *Washington Post* Folk Festival Committee—featured Eleanor Roosevelt as honorary chairman. Twenty-eight senators were named as committee members, along with cabinet members and scores of other Washington luminaries. Participants numbered in the hundreds and came from as many as thirty states.

Fostering interactions of folk artists, folklorists, folkies, and general audiences, these and the thousands of folk festivals patterned after them seem to have changed the world slightly more than it has changed them. Sarah Gertrude Knott sent these words to George Korson on the eve of his directing the first Pennsylvania Folk Festival:

> The things we are doing seem so real to me, I believe we are striking right down at the very depths of something. It is a strange thing how we get these ideas and strong urges, which I believe amount to inspiration, and how "hell and high water" cannot stop us. We do not make any money out of it, we have all kinds of battles to fight, and nobody sees why we are fighting, but there is something inside us that pushes us on. When there is accomplishment it is more to us than those on

the outside, and so I quite understand the feelings you have in seeing your dreams come true, and you are truly doing a marvelous thing.

*With grateful appreciation to the Folklore Archives, Western Kentucky University, and to Angus K. Gillespie, James W. Wilson, Mike Joyce, and Jack Pickering.*

# Folk Festivals

## *History, Concepts, Definitions*

*with Lee Udall*

### THE PROCESS AND MATERIAL OF FOLKLORE

Culture at all levels is both conservative and creative. Today's culture is largely received from yesterday, and even in times of rapid innovation there are several times as many cultural items being transmitted from the past as being newly devised. Language, for example, is an aspect of culture subject to constant revision, but the larger part is handed through the generations. We learn to speak it as it comes to us from the people who have spoken it before us.

But while each of us may learn the larger part of language in much the same way, culture is transmitted and controlled differently by groups. In a modern industrial society such as the United States, three major levels comprise the overall culture. These have sometimes been visualized as a layer cake—although an ice cream sandwich might be more appropriate, as the middle layer is larger than the top or bottom layers.

The top layer is academic culture. It is largely formal, highly organized, and controlled by relatively small, elite groups. It has governmental

---

Excerpted from chapter one of *Folk Festivals: A Handbook for Organization and Management*, by Joe Wilson and Lee Udall, copyright 1982 by the University of Tennessee Press: Knoxville.

and institutional support. It is transmitted through conservatories, graduate schools, libraries, and other institutions of education. It is Longfellow's poems, a symphony, an opera, a formal play, and other fine arts. It is written history and other elements of the humanities.

The middle layer is popular culture. It is disseminated and controlled by many individuals and by major industries, including those devoted to publishing, film, radio, television, and recording. It is transmitted through the mass media and supported by sales. It is popular magazines, the songs of Stephen Foster, soap opera, advertising art, graphic prints, and comics.

The bottom layer is folk culture. It is informal, noncommercial, and usually transmitted orally in face-to-face situations and in small groups. It changes continually because it is shaped by the memories, creative abilities, and needs of human beings in particular situations. It is of the group, but the touch of the individual is on each item. A song may be traditional, but an individual may vary the nuance, the melody, voice timbre, a word, or a line.

Each of us has participated in all three levels of culture and will continue to do so. We relate anecdotes and stories passed to us orally, share group experiences and assumptions, watch television, read magazines, visit art galleries, and enjoy ballet.

What part does a folk festival have in the cultural processes? First, it should be understood that festivals cannot present very much of folk culture. Culture is ideas, behaviors, attitudes, and much more that is resistant to presentation, so it is futile to expect folk festivals to show much of the beauty and depth of folk culture. Festivals present performers and products out of context, and the products best received are those developed as performing arts by the groups that evolved them.

## A CONFUSION REGARDING FOLK CULTURE

A problem central to choosing participants and conducting a folk festival is a nationwide confusion regarding what folk culture is. This confusion is fed by large, well-established sales industries—publishing companies, the commercial music industry, music schools, touring agencies, Chambers of Commerce, and even the scriptwriters for television series. Popular cult figures such as Bob Dylan and Joan Baez are considered folksingers, and forms of pseudo-folklore are created to sell breakfast cereal.

Confusion also stems from so-called "folk festivals," which have long existed without conceptual and aesthetic standards for distinguishing between traditional folk performers and the various categories of nontraditional performers who sing "folksongs" and call themselves "folksingers." An authentic folk artist seldom uses such terms; he is likely to describe himself as a Cajun musician, a Ukrainian musician, a blacksmith, a white oak basketmaker, or another similarly specific term.

Some early producers of folk festivals hoped they could sort folk performers from popular performers simply by not paying anyone, and requiring that performed items be of the folk tradition. Alas, it is not so easy. Elements of folk culture are performed by persons who are not part of those cultures, the folk borrow items from popular culture, and most people wish to be paid when they perform at festivals. There is nothing wrong with persons of other traditions borrowing and using folklore, but a singer of folksongs is not a folksinger unless his performance has been cast in the processes by which the folk develop art. Most people do not bother with such distinctions and unquestioningly accept items of popular culture ascribed to the folk, but directors of folk festivals need to draw careful distinctions.

The crucial touchstone for those who wish to engage in dignified and reasonably accurate presentations is *oral transmission and variability within a group*. One may find folklore that does not appear to be orally transmitted, but even in such cases closer examination will usually show that the item is largely shaped through oral tradition. An example is Sacred Harp singing. The Sacred Harp is a hymnal, in use since 1844, whose notation uses the shape of notes in addition to their place on the staff to indicate pitch. Rural "singing school" teachers of the Southeast and Southwest teach this form of notation in two- and three-week sessions. The use of book and teacher would seem to define this as academic art. A closer analysis reveals, however, that much of the transmission process is oral and aural. A person who purchases a copy of the Sacred Harp can learn the pitch of notes from it, but the *style* of singing is not clear from the notes. In fact, no common system of notation could convey the style. Who are these "singing school" teachers? They are rural preachers, farmers, mechanics, carpenters, and others whose education usually stopped at some point in the secondary level. Their skills were learned in church, at all-day singings, and in earlier "singing schools."

Let's look at the major types of performers who describe themselves or are described by others as folk performers.

Performers reared in the culture from which the performed materials are drawn include:

1. *Traditional folk performers*. While acculturation is pervasive and affects all, these performers are those who tend to hold closest to their culture's traditional forms and styles of performance. They are guided by the aesthetic of the group that produced the performed material and are not self-conscious in performing this material. The material may be changed or varied, but only within the aesthetic of the group which produced it. Such performers may know of other forms and styles, but it would probably not occur to them to adopt these styles. They may occasionally adapt material from outside the culture, but they still hold to the group aesthetic in performing it. Their presentation is usually within the group or community and is an accepted part of other activities rather than an event in itself—one performs at weddings, christenings, auctions, funerals, dances, and feast days rather than at concerts of the arts.
2. *Aware traditional performers*. Such performers are much like the above, in that the material performed and the style of the performance is largely based upon the group aesthetic. Like traditional folk performers, they also hold to traditional forms and are unlikely to blend them with other forms not approved by the group. They differ in that the unself-conscious quality is gone; they may be aware that what they perform is "folk art," and they may regularly perform outside the group or community which produced the form. Realizing that folk art buffs prize authenticity, they may return to older forms and materials which the group has abandoned.
3. *Evolved traditional performers*. Again, the personal roots of the performers are in folk tradition, but the aesthetic and materials of the dominant culture have largely supplanted those of the group. Such performers may work full-time at their art. They tend to be highly conscious of the styles in which they perform and of other forms, and they may blend forms. The material performed tends to be idiosyncratic, although the flavor and style of the group which produced it may be an obvious and prized part of the performance. Some of these performers draw materials from popular cultural sources, such as radio and television, and adapt it to local tastes.

Performers who adopt elements of style and materials from cultures in which they were not reared:

1. *Performers* who reproduce traditional folk styles. Some performers attempt to reproduce material found in folk culture stitch-by-stitch and note-by-note, while others closely adhere to form and style but stop short of actual copying. This type of performer is found most often in folk music, and such performers usually have as their models recordings made by traditional folk artists. In the case of musicians and dancers, it is not unusual for an individual performer to present works created in several cultures, holding closely to the form or style of forms as disparate as old-time Appalachian string band music and Delta blues music. Such performers are highly selective in borrowing elements of folk culture, seldom adopting anything more than performing style. They may sing the songs of evangelical Baptists, but they are not likely to become part of a group of evangelical Baptists; their culture is usually the contemporary dominant culture.
2. Performers who innovate upon adopted folk styles. There is a wide range of performers in this category. They differ from those described above in that while they may use such words as "folk" and "traditional," they are more concerned with individual creativity than with the adopted styles upon which they base their creations. They are less likely to have specific traditional folk artists as models, and their works of art are more likely to be individualistic. As in the case of others who adopt elements of folk style, the culture of these performers is likely to be of the contemporary dominant culture.
3. Performers who create in folk-like style. There is only a hint of folk style in such performers, and the material performed is likely to be of the artist's making. This hint of folk style may be subtle: the use of a guitar while singing, the singing of coal-mining songs, or the use of salt glaze on pottery. Nevertheless, performers in this category are the pop-folk, singer-songwriter, cult figures and craft shop operators who are most likely to be described as "folksingers" or "folk artists" by the mass media. The materials and styles of such artists are, in fact, a part of popular culture.

At the outset—before you retain any performers—establish a policy on whether your festival will present persons who have adopted performance elements of a folk culture, as well as traditional folk performers, and, if so, which kind of performer will predominate. This decision should be treated with care; no other issue has so divided scholars in this field from those who have presented festivals.

# Preserving the Universe

Among the folk, there is little art for art's sake. A quilt may reflect a group aesthetic for proper quiltmaking, and its making may be a pleasing creative outlet, but its function is to warm its owner. A weathervane pleases the eye, but its function is to show the direction of the wind. A pie safe may be art, but its function is to prevent flies from settling on pies and pastries while they cool.

Folklore is functional, and much of it is very complex. Riddles puzzle and amuse, but they also teach logic. Many of the best-loved American folk hymns have the function of preparing the singer for death, always a chief concern of religion. A folk proverb may contain the compacted wisdom of a people in dealing with a common problem. The singing of

---

From *Center for Southern Folklore Newsletter*, Volume 2, Number 2, Summer, 1979. Joe Wilson wrote: "Many small magazines were founded in the '70s, and this first appeared in a magazine with a folk arts focus that our pal Bill Ferris sent [Dr. William R. Ferris, who later served as chairman of the National Endowment for the Humanities, co-founded the Center for Southern Folklore and was its director from 1972 to 1984.] It said that tradition was not weak, and that it might continue despite serious attack. The article is a favorite of my wife Kathy, who kept a copy for years."

a bloody ballad may function to reinforce mores by pointing to the dire results of aberrant behavior.

Although their function may be obscure to persons outside a culture, folk rituals are also functional. "We observe our ancient customs," the Eskimo headman told Rasmussen, "so that the universe may be preserved." A ritual with a function that important is not easily abandoned.

On the night of May 3, 1939, Theodore White was in Chunking [now spelled Chongqing], China, when that city was subjected to the first mass bombing in the history of the world to be aimed at a civilian population. He wrote:

> The town was built of bamboo and wood. And it burned and burned and it screamed—you could hear the flames roaring. When the raid was over, that was the night of an eclipse of the moon. According to ancient Chinese tradition, the eclipse happens when the Dog of Heaven tries to gobble up the moon. They have to scare the dog off by beating on gongs. There were the peasants in Chunking, trapped. The Japanese were attacking from above, there were air-raid sirens, and yet they had to scare off the Dog of Heaven from eating up the moon. I remember the sounds of their gongs in the night—beating and beating—and the sounds of the gongs mixing with the wailing and crying of the wounded and terror-sticken.[1]

Other writers who have described Chinese traditions associated with a lunar eclipse have used terms such as "charming pageant," "quaint ritual," and "an excuse for a noisy celebration." But Theodore White was witness to the fact that the exercise of such traditions is much more than a superficial matter.

A few of the indigenous folk festivals in the U.S. are older than the nation. They have continued because their functions have continued to be relevant in the cultures which created and sustain them, and because they have sufficient internal flexibility to deal with change in those cultures. The Fiesta de Santa Fe, which began in 1712 as a Spanish village fiesta, continues in modern Santa Fe. One of its major functions is common to many other older festivals: tension is relieved through a suspension of the normal rules of behavior. In Santa Fe, the beginning of the fiesta is signaled by the classic device of burning Zozobra (Old Man Gloom) and the revelry begins. Some Santa Fe antiquarians harrumph that it is no longer traditional, due to the inclusion of non-Spanish materials. Yet most of the revelers appear to be working-class people of Spanish and Mexican ancestry. Many of the Santa Fe bourgeoisie stay home and complain that the fiesta has become a drunken revel, seemingly unaware that this is traditional and perhaps even the central function of this festival.

It is ironic that the oldest folk festivals in the U.S. are usually not called folk festivals. During the past forty years, this term has been preempted by other kinds of events, which remove items of folklore from their functional contexts and present them in new contexts, most often to non-folk audiences with antiquarian interests. We were not the first to do this, nor even the first to realize that such an act changes function. Emperor K'ang-Hsi of China (1661–1722) wrote:

> Many people, after all, call old porcelain vessels "antiques," but if we think of vessels from the view of principle, then we know that once they were meant to be used. Only now are they grubby-looking and unsuitable for us to drink from, so we end up putting them on our desks or on bookshelves, and look at them once in a while. On the other hand, we can change the function of a given object and thus change its nature, as I did by converting a rustless sword that the Dutch once gave me into a measuring stick that I kept on my desk.[2]

But what is the function of these new festivals, which present folk arts to audiences which are largely not of the cultures which produced these arts? First, the rise of cultural consumerism is obviously involved because we use the word "audience." In the community-based indigenous folk festival, audience and performer are often so interwoven as to be impossible to view as separate entities. Even at the older fiddlers' conventions, such as the one held annually at Galax, Virginia, the audience and performers are closely interwoven. It is only the tourists who sit in the stands and watch the stage proceedings. The traditional audience is scattered throughout the field and parking lots, gathered in tight clusters around groups of musicians, drinking, dancing, and calling out requests.

Second, it is obvious that these new festivals grow from a different level of consciousness of folk art. The organizers are sophisticates rather than folk. This consciousness seems to arise when a group—or self-appointed advocates of a group—feels its culture is disappearing. At this point, attempts are made to preserve it. These range from recording or filming portions of it, to the holding of festivals, or the creation of an edifice which will serve as a museum for its artifactual record. Of course, these attempts invariably fail to preserve the culture.

Artifacts are important, but they are only the dry bones of a culture. Films entertain and enlighten, but they are the shadow of reality. Festivals expand consciousness and involve their audiences with the folk in the flesh, but they cannot encapsulate or reproduce the life of the folk. Cultures change for complex social and economic reasons, and the forces which fuel these changes are much more powerful than the feeble attempts of those who speak of preservation as a possibility. Even if preservation were possible, it would be both controversial and dangerous.

These new festivals are K'ang-Hsi's measuring stick rather than his sword. The basketmaker may make baskets in exactly the same manner as her grandfather, but she sells them to tourists who will use them as decorative art rather than to farm women for gathering eggs. The Baptists who sing "Why not tonight?" at a festival are not likely to save any souls. The form has continued but the function has changed.

What are the real functions of these new festivals for the folk who present their arts? First, they validate these arts as arts. Like others in our society, the folk recognize the validation implicit in a call to perform at the White House or at a major event. Second, they strengthen concepts of value attached to the art and the efforts which produce it. Our society has tended to erode such concepts among the folk by means which have been both deliberate and artificial.

But what is the function of these new festivals for city audiences who largely (and erroneously) feel they are seeing the arts of rural and urban isolates? At one level, they function to preserve an illusion. City dwellers have long believed that rural life is marked by the retention of moral values and virtues that are lost in the evil and impersonality of the city. This illusion goes at least as far back as the Bible, when shepherds were men of exemplary virtue. (They had the honor of welcoming Jesus, while wise men were being sent to pay tribute.)

The virtues of the village and farm have been extolled for centuries and such beliefs have been factors in establishing national economic policy. This is true even today in the United States, where agricultural policy is based upon supporting the family farm despite the opposition of many economists. Although illusion dies hard, anthropologists and folklorists have found that the folk are good and bad in roughly the same proportion as other people.

There is a more important function for audiences, and it has nothing to do with illusion. Folk festivals present an attractive alternative to the bland homogeneity of most of the arts produced by those who must put profits ahead of all other considerations. For those who reject commercial art but put Western European art upon a pedestal, they can demonstrate that local aesthetic standards and creativity exist in genres other than the chosen few. For the underfunded local arts council engaged in aping the cultural offering of New York, they offer a practical solution. The time will come when even arts council directors realize that a good bluesman is better than a bad symphony.

NOTES

1. Theodore H. White and Mel Stuart, *China: The Roots of Madness; a Documentary* (New York: Norton, 1968).
2. Jonathan D. Spence, *Emperor of China: Self-Portrait of K'ang-Hsi* (New York: Vintage Books, 1975).

# Confessions of a Folklorist

Please allow me to introduce myself.

I'm the devil incarnate, the folklorist who stopped booking the Highwoods String Band at that ultimate status-conferring event, the National Folk Festival. That was fourteen years ago, and I'm totally unrepentant and absolutely certain it was the right thing to do.

---

This is an abridged version of Joe Wilson's article in *Old-Time Music* magazine, Spring 1990 (2.3), about which Joe said, "It was a response to an article written by Mac Benford of the Highwoods String Band. My programming decisions for booking the National Folk Festival at the time leaned heavily toward the remaining pioneers. Mac thought Highwoods should continue to be on the festival. My response set forth an aesthetic at variance with his, and pissed off more people than the income tax."

Folklore scholar Neil Rosenberg provides further background:

> *The Old-Time Herald* started in the fall of 1987, publishing eight issues a year during its first five years. In 1989, it began a regular column: "Issues in Old-Time Music," and the first article there was Mac Benford's "Folklorists & Us: An Account of Our Curious and Changing Relationship (with More Personal Reminiscences)" (*OTH* 1.7 Feb.–Apr. 89: 22–27). A debate about revivalists in old-time music ensued in the column's letters and articles. I wrote about this in *Transforming Tradition* (Urbana: University of Illinois Press, 1993, pp.181–82), stating in a footnote: "For over a year every issue of the magazine following the appearance of Benford's piece carried letters about the topic, and Wilson's piece prompted a fresh flood; the debate continues as this is written."

Mac Benford [banjoist and singer with the Highwoods String Band, 1972–1979] is still singing the same "song" he did when he visited me in 1976. He is saying that folklorists have not helped him and other tradition-borrowers to become professional musicians. In my case he is right. We have very different ideas of what my job is.

He says that being booked on the National and Smithsonian festivals helped his group obtain jobs. He believes I should plan the National Folk Festival with an eye to providing those selected with entries for their résumés and clippings for their press kits. But the option is more mine than his, and that is not what I choose to do.

Mac's account of folkie travails in the late seventies tries to find a culprit for changes that eroded professional opportunities in old-time music. He offers folklorists as the evildoers in his scenario, in a mental process that is reminiscent of the pulp mystery where one begins to suspect the poor butler on the third page. In fact, the old-time music boomlet closed down on cue with the rest of what has been called "the great folk music scare of the sixties." There came a day when people who had been generally supportive were not as interested as they had been. There are mornings when the nation gets up and changes its mind.

Mac sometimes invents positions for folklorists then bops them. I can't imagine any folklorist claiming to be a dispassionate scientist. But I do know some that despise all folk music, and feel that it is the hair on the tip of the tail of the dog of folk studies that tries to wag the whole animal. Most of the 1,100 members of the American Folklore Society have nothing at all to do with folk music. They know little or nothing about it and are likely to remain disinterested. Those interested in it to the point of doing any serious work in music are fifty or less—the exact number depending upon how seriously one defines "serious."

Ethnomusicologists are more concerned with folk music than folklorists, and are increasingly a presence in arts organizations all over the country—though I don't know anyone of that persuasion who is much interested in old-time music. A real steel-belted, six-ply folklorist teaches at the university level, does research, feels some pressure to publish, and hopes for a sabbatical every seven years in order to do something interesting.

So I urge any of you who have been irritated at folklorists to recognize that they have not wronged you. A few of our pedagogic brethren in that profession may like folk music, but most are no more likely to promote its performance than an entomologist is likely to promote better treatment for fleas.

Here's a major confession: there's never been a time when folklorists were a majority of the programming committee that selects artists for the National Folk Festival. The people who serve on that committee, including folklorists, have this in common: most are revival musicians. At one point in the early eighties, there were seven banjoists on the NCTA board, all but one performing in old-time styles. No one planned to have that many banjoists on the board—it just happened.

Here's another confession: I'm not really a folklorist. Folklorists are members of an academic discipline, and I'm terribly undisciplined—no good at university departmental politics, and a failure at conceptual thinking. I go through entire days without defining anything. I have been reading books written by folklorists for over thirty years, and dabbling in their pond, but I've never loitered at a university long enough for them to invite me to engage in that rite of passage where mortarboards are worn and sheep hides distributed, with the participants becoming what one of my mountain friends calls "talking doctors." I think they'd let me be a folklorist if I would submit my head for two or three years of probing and stuffing, but there's a part of me that prefers being the red-headed stepchild in the family. Nobody expects much of you, so there's always a chance you can offer a happy surprise.

Until recently, people who worked off-campus—especially those without advanced degrees—were called *amateur* folklorists. Being somewhat retrograde in my thinking, I like that category better than the others, and if I ever give up my red-headed stepchild tag and promote myself as a folklorist, that's the kind I want to be. I like being associated with well-intentioned potential bunglers.

Mac mentions me by job in 1976: "the prospective director of the NCTA," and recalls "providing input." The "input" was that Mac and others thought the organization that employs me should become a booking agency for Highwoods and other performing groups. Mac said, "We just want to earn our living at this, the way Gid and Riley and those guys did." I was dumbfounded, so taken aback that the phrase has remained intact in my memory.

What stunned me was that Mac didn't know that Gid Tanner was a chicken farmer, Clayton McMichen an automobile mechanic, and that Riley Puckett did a blind man's act on the street with a tin cup. They didn't make a living from being the Skillet Lickers. Mac had assimilated the sound from those old 78s, but the players of that music remained as remote as if they had lived on the other side of the moon. They'd become a romantic vision—cheery fellows who tootled about the South making a good living playing old-time music.

Has any old-time musician ever earned a living playing instrumental music? One can point to the Carter Family, the Mainers, Uncle Dave [Macon], Jimmie Rodgers, Fiddlin' John Carson, and a few others, but their living came from vocals or showmanship.

When folk arts apprenticeships were invented a few years back, Kathy James [Joe Wilson's wife, a public sector folklorist and photographer at the time] wondered if it might be a good idea for the young learners to also learn the trades of their master teachers. "The people who are learning from Dewey (Balfa) should learn to drive a school bus, and those Tommy (Jarrell) is teaching should learn how to scrape a gravel road and make moonshine," she said. "We'd have great music and lots of bright young barbers."

I thought it a funny comment then, but now it seems almost profound. The new set of values says that it is better to be a professional artist than a good barber who happens to be the best fiddler in town. Is it? I asked the opinion of former Kentucky coal miner and present Tennessee hog and cattle farmer—and very fine fiddler—Kenny Baker. "Put me down on the side of good barbers," Kenny said.

Mac seems to think that lots of government money is being spent on folk music and he is concerned about getting his part. [But in fact] most of the "government" money spent on folk music goes to revival performers. Every year I see twenty or more brochures which show the touring performers that regional and state arts agencies are supporting. Virtually all are from the revival. I have never been concerned to the point of counting, but it is at least ninety percent—perhaps more. It is the same with the Folk Music in the Schools programs. Revival performers can cope with the bureaucracy, and they get all the jobs. Nor does the situation differ when park and recreation departments hire folk musicians. Almost all the public money I see being spent on folk music goes to revival performers.

While I'm getting Mac straightened out about funding, I'll deny his assertion that my employer, the National Council for the Traditional Arts (NCTA), is "coordinating government tours and festivals." The NCTA is a private non-profit organization. We've organized fifteen national tours in the last ten years, paying our way with whatever federal, state, local, and private grants we could attract, and with a lot of local sponsors and box-office income. The biggest source of funds for us and for the local sponsors is, of course, the box office.

Here's another confession: the National Folk Festival never stopped booking revivalists. Revivalists of one kind or another have been booked on all fifty-one festivals. But Mac is right, there was a major policy change, and it amounted to more than withdrawing the invitation to Highwoods. Basically, it was a decision to put a much greater emphasis upon the traditional, to get as close to the original as possible, to present the rare rather than the commonplace.

There's a perfectly fine replica of the Parthenon in Centennial Park in Nashville, Tennessee. The glory that was Greece is beautifully kept on a manicured green, the columns all standing and the roof intact. Yet few come to see this exercise in civic pride. But there's no want for visitors at the site of the ancient wreck in Athens. Standing on that hillside, one is awed by concepts that arose from tribalism. How on earth did hardscrabble farmers, open-boat fishermen, and keepers of sheep and goats conceive and create at an architectural level that has dazzled men for more than two thousand years? One feels affinity, sympathy, a closeness. Is it possible to feel close to a concrete company and architectural copycats in Nashville?

Are we the only arts presenters who prefer originals? Are we singular in preferring the rare? There's a German painter, recently released from a prison term for forgery, who can imitate the style of any of a half-dozen famous European painters to a degree that defies detection by respected specialists. One could make a scrapbook of the certificates of authenticity that experts have issued to his fakes. Is this dabbler admired and revered for his considerable skill? He is not. A British critic cans him as, "execrable scum, a copy machine, a hand linked to an eye without passing through a brain."

Yes, we know that traditional arts exist along a continuum, that even the most traditional artist has made choices that reflect an evolution.

So why do we prefer the less evolved? There are at least three good reasons. One is justice. The most original artists in our world of art tend to be hidden from view. You can see everything else labeled "folk," but it is hard to see the originals.

Second, this is where we are needed. The rest of the great array of artists labeled "folk" tend to take good care of themselves. There are, of course, complaints from artists who try to work as folk professionals, but they are much like the complaints one hears from other professional musicians—which is to say they are reasonable complaints but there is no special case for advocacy in them.

Third, virtually all presentations that are labeled "folk" have dropped the less-evolved in favor of artists who are of the revival or—more likely—popular. All pressures on those who present are to make everything look and sound like everything else. "Purist" is the common pejorative for anyone who resists. In more than thirty years of doing work like this, I can't recall anyone ever asking for more purity. Everyone wants less, but only until they get it. Then the event looks like all the rest, and is boring and dies without anyone noticing.

The revivalists found at the National in recent years have most often been Asians, Africans, and performers of various minority arts: American Indian dancers, klezmer musicians, and more. Revivalism is easier for our programming committee to accept when the originals are very distant or very rare. Are we inconsistent? We are. We hold to a slightly higher standard of authenticity in selecting Anglo American and African American artists than we do when the artists are from the Pacific Rim, Africa, or Latin America.

Am I troubled by all this? Not much. Consistency is a trait as overrated as virginity and nearly as useless. Whenever anyone suggests that all the very different people who wear the labels "folk," "traditional," or even "old-time" should start pulling in the same direction, you can be certain that that person is either terribly idealistic or as dumb as a shovel. I think it is fine for us all to go off in different directions. I choose what to do with my life, and have no suggestions about what you do with yours.

All programming is, of course, discriminatory. What in hell else could it be? Some are chosen and others are left unpicked on the vine for the bugs. Is that fair? Of course not. If you must have a group to blame for being left on the vine, with bugs chewing on your backside, feel free to resent red-headed stepchildren. Rejection is a terrible thing, and the only good that ever comes from it is songwriting royalties, self-understanding, and second marriages.

I suppose we seem terribly perverse, because it is not only the sound that is being judged, but the family tree—past and future—of the people making it. That violates precepts that most educated Americans revere as much as they do motherhood. Here the race is not to the swiftest, nor honors to the student that raised his hand most often. The one who has worked hardest is not automatically promoted, and the brightest is not necessarily considered the best. Here there's a terrible perversion of conventional Americanism, and the social register is used for doggie paper.

What seems to irritate people most is our denial of the central religious tenet of the intellectual portion of the great American middle class. Their religion is art, and we deny that access to an area of art can be bought. There's no difficulty in buying your way into most arts circles. If you wish to be punk, you buy a tube of wax, put your hair into five spikes, and spray them with green paint. You buy skin-tight black vinyl pants, a red vest, three chains, pointy-toed boots, a safety pin for your ear, an electronic keyboard, and five punk records. You've paid your money and you are punk from the first day. No one will ever question it.

Some try to buy being folk with another uniform: DeKalb Corn or John Deere cap, overalls, clodhopper shoes, faded shirt, open-back banjo or factory fiddle, and all of Tommy Jarrell's records. You put on the uniform, buy a road atlas detailed enough to show Galax or Mount Airy, and go there. The gentle folks thereabouts will accept any waif that wanders in, and musical ones are especially treasured.

It seems a harmless process. If one is dissatisfied with the family that fate gave him, it is OK to adopt another. But fairness demands that one be more than a young cuckoo. Do you know the ingrate habits of that bird that Tom Ashley sang about? The cuckoo lays its eggs in the nests of other birds and they unwittingly raise its young. The noisy and aggressive young cuckoo often pushes its nestmates—the natural offspring of its adoptive parents—over the side, out of the nest, and to death. A hard corollary? Yes, it is—very hard and applicable only to a few. But there really are ethical considerations in learning traditional skills, combining them with non-traditional skills (such as self-advertising), and going into competition with traditional people.

Those sensitive enough to wish to avoid young cuckoo habits could start by not squawking about there being a few places reserved for the originals of our world of art, for the carriers of tradition. They could also organize their thinking and rely less on imagination in locating their place in this world of art. There's a revivalist tendency to invent an impossibly romantic theory about folk music, pass it back and forth as a formulation from anonymous folklorists—then, at an appropriate moment—to do a skinhead baseball bat attack upon the theory and folklorists in general.

A good example is the "isolated mountain community" theory for the development and continuation of style in old-time music. "They're all gone now!" we hear; suddenly there are no isolated places or people. Any old retrograde geezer chugging down the interstate is a last gasp ahead of the actuary, and probably can't hold a crowd with his performance standards. There's a self-serving summary: "They're dead; we're it."

Mac believes that isolation once kept people distinct, but that it has ended, and that blob culture now takes over. He says, "People can no longer be born into culturally distinct isolated geographic areas. They just don't exist. We are now all part of the homogenized blend, like it or not." In these and other comments, Mac reveals himself as an evangelist for the *plasticus boobus americanus* cult. His family and his community became culturally mainstream; Mac found the water terribly tepid and perhaps even a bit polluted. That is evidence of good taste, but Mac is over his head in the mainstream and can't imagine other fluids, such as duck soup, sheep-nanny tea, and home brew with raisins.

Mac is sometimes wonderfully evangelical. He says, " . . . we are the ones through which (sic) the tradition is now flowing. We are the link between its past and its future and there is no other. If old-time music is played in the twenty-first century, it will be because of us, and this will be as true in the rural South as anywhere else."

Jeez, old friend, I hate to rain on your parade, but I think it is also flowing through the Indians of the sub-arctic, and I have more faith in their grandchildren continuing it than I do in yours. The Athabascan Indians of the interior and north of Alaska received mail only twice a year during the 1920s and 1930s, but they could send furs to Sears Roebuck, and they could receive crank-up phonographs, records, fiddles and guitars. Now they have a great fiddlers' convention every November, flying into Fairbanks from the upriver and downriver Yukon villages, some from north of the Arctic Circle in Alaska, and others from Canada's most remote reaches.

The tune heard most often from the stage in the cozy Fairbanks Eagles Hall is "More Pretty Girls Than One," derived from the 1930s Arthur Smith recording. The recorded repertoire of Mainer's Mountaineers is also well known. These and other early hillbilly items are mixed with old tunes from the early fur trade. The fiddlers from Arctic Village and Old Crow (Canada) clog their feet in the Quebec manner, and the Old Crow guitar players clog along with the fiddler.

The second most common tune is "The Red River Jig," a favorite dance and tune of the fur trade. It is well known among Michif Indian fiddlers of North Dakota's Turtle Mountain Reservation, descendants of the Cree and Chippewa who were the foot soldiers of the fur trade. Athabascan Indian old-time fiddlers also play Scottish tunes learned from Hudson Bay employees of long ago, a few French tunes, and lots of items from 1920s-to-Hank Williams country music. The last of the great North American primeval hunting tribes, they neither sow nor gather; fish are for dogs, and men hunt and eat meat. They are among the several groups of "no others" the tradition is flowing through, but don't worry about slighting them. They've not heard about Highwoods, or any other revival bands, so you're even.

My world of old-time music has many players in a variety of traditional forms, in many places, and is in a state of robust health. No one worries about commercializing it, and the fifties and eighties seem as important as the twenties and sixties. I see revivalists too, and there are some good musicians among them, but they just don't seem that all-fired important nor numerous in a qualitative sense. I'd guess there are more really good old-time fiddlers playing right now in the state of Missouri than there have been good revival fiddlers in the entire country in the twentieth century.

The largest group of "no others" the string band tradition is flowing through is the same group it has always flowed through. They may pick up a non-folk item from popular performance, the revival, or the church, but they make it their own and they can digest a lot of what the great musicologist Charles Seeger called "nonfolkness." The folk have swallowed whole genres of popular music without even burping.

Getting stuck in one place is as dangerous for styles as for tunes. Close imitation is a creative black hole. The best that the artist can create amounts to nothing more than a moment already past—perhaps a beautiful moment well worth remembering, but surely not worthy of fixative worship. Items from folk culture may have value after death. There are a few people in every age who learn from dry bones in glass cases, from the shadows of what once was on film, from field recordings, and the reports of scholars housed in museums and archives. But the cemeteries of a culture are always distant from its birthing places, and there's not much communication.

We are not the only people who have to struggle with these issues. My friend Jill was, for a time, lawyer for the Museum of New Mexico. One of the museum's sites is the ancient Palace of the Governors in Santa Fe. For generations, Indians from various pueblos have sat in the plaza at the front of the Palace, selling handmade jewelry. A few years ago, non-Indian makers of handmade jewelry wished to sell from that site. But the museum said this public place was reserved for an Indian tradition. There was a lawsuit, and the museum won its case of Indian arts advocacy.

There's much glib generalizing nowadays about what is called "cultural conservation," but the term precedes any real process or definition. It is a catch phrase created for grants committees and budget planners, and reflects the flimsiness of sloganeering, the petty posturing of applicants and boosters. When our most-respected public institutions are asked to preserve, they still must respond with embalming. We've learned how to pickle King Tut, and how to keep the right amount of humidity around the stuff he had, and that is progress. Perhaps in the next century, we will get beyond mummification and imitation, and become as adept at easing the transitions of life as we are those of death.

Can we get really honest with each other and admit that old-time is a part of folk music, and thus the property of the lower classes? Yes, I know that in this great republic it is considered terribly unpatriotic to admit that there is more than one class, even though the term "middle" presupposes the existence of upper and lower classes. But I think I have the right. I come from a family in one of those lower classes, born in a two-room house at the head of an Appalachian hollow, with no electricity and no running water. My mother was nineteen when I was born, and I was a second son. She sang ballads she'd learned from her grandmother, and my dad was the tenor in a gospel quartet and a good harmonica player. Among the uncles, aunts, and cousins there were fiddlers, banjoists, and guitarists.

Mac speaks of having " . . . had the poor fortune to be separated by age and geography from the older Southern musicians." Age is not an important factor in his separation from the culture, and region matters very little. Most of the really good traditional musicians I meet are younger than he is, and sweat-stained people exist everywhere and always have. Only a pedant would ask that they be defined. They do not remain fixed in time as performing-arts museums, and they define tradition as they move with it. Sometimes they let old things die, and that is OK, if it is time for that old thing to die.

I find it ironic that Mac does not know how fortunate he was to be born into the great American middle class. I'm even suspicious that he is pulling our crank in saying he admires older Southern mountain culture. He never became part of that culture, but he could have. If he had by now spent twenty-five years on the Piper's Gap Road near Galax, he'd be nearly indistinguishable from other Grayson County residents. But learning 150 tunes in a style does not open a culture. Do the brass band members in the New Orleans 7th Ward welcome the white-boy jazzmen from Omaha as long-lost brothers whenever they blow into town, knowing many of the same tunes? Do Plains Indians give barbecues to honor the Boy Scouts who have become expert in rendering Indian dances?

They do not. Folk and tribal people tend to be cordial, but brotherhood is more than 150 tunes in a style. You have to be more, stay longer, and absorb some of what caused the creation of the artistry. You can't make a good pickle by squirting vinegar on a cucumber. It has to soak awhile.

The political essence of revivalism is found in populism, an assumption that points to the superiority of an earlier age. It looks backward and longs for a lost agrarian Eden—when the laborer had good prospects, the farmer had abundance, there were no beggars, people sang around a campfire, and a nearly flawless common endowment of rich resources was held in lands, minerals, and culture. It says that we have but to throw off the present errors and become unified to regain this lost Eden.

It stems from an ancient urban belief that virtue and quality are first given to basic people, that the veneers of civilization mask more than they reveal, and that open spaces and hard work build character. It is found in many cultures and is timeless. The star blazed over the most humble abode in Bethlehem, a stable. The couple was poverty-stricken, and poor shepherds were given the honor of welcoming, while wise men had to travel far and pay tribute.

Mac says that, in gathering material for his article, he found stories "ranging from the amusing to the infuriating, reflecting the current attitude of the folklorists towards so-called 'revivalists.'" Well, I can't tell stories for the folklorists, but I have a few anecdotes of my own. I came to my job after years of interacting with serious collectors and learners, who took pride in accuracy and had considerable regard for the truth.

I was in my first week at the NCTA when I noticed the record, picture, and press-release blurb for Marie. She was beautiful—a *Vogue* model with a fiddle. The blurb said that she was a fiddler, but classically trained, and could "fiddle the socks off most old-time fiddlers." I've had a long acquaintance with old-time fiddlers. I've met Charlie Bowman, Arthur Smith, Pappy McMichen, Clark Kessinger, and Benny Thomasson. If Marie could fiddle their socks off, she had to be great. I put the record on the turntable with considerable anticipation. Early in the first side it became obvious that either the old-time fiddlers in Marie's neighborhood were in a terribly weakened condition or her blurb writer was deaf.

Other disappointments followed. An audition cassette from a band on the coast found its way to my desk, and I found it amazing. These folks were playing tunes from a Tommy Jarrell album, in the same order that they appeared on side one of the record. I knew the order because I'd helped choose it, cutting up the tape and putting in the paper leader. A few days later a manager-performer telephoned me. Here's how I recall what was said.

"Yes, ma'am, I did get your cassette and it is very nice. You're coming along fine, getting a good string-band sound, so keep on doing it."

"So you'll hire us for the National Folk Festival?"

"Well, ma'am, we hire just one old-time band for the festival. It is not an old-time festival or country music festival. We have to cover lots of bases, many very different ethnic and regional musics, and we're planning to hire Tommy Jarrell this year, and I know you would not want to compete with him . . ."

(Interrupting) "Why not? You call it a national festival, but it looks very skewed to the East to me. You need to hire some people from out here—get some regional balance."

"Are you telling me that your band wants to compete with Tommy, playing his music?"

"Oh, come on. He doesn't own the music. He got it from somebody too, didn't he? It is an international music now, not just a little localized sound. He may be a link in a chain, but we are too, and a link beyond him. You need to have a broader program. You've had bands from that little area for years, now you need to represent the places it has spread to."

"Do you think I'll be able to find a Monterey Jack cheese maker in West Virginia?"

"I don't understand."

"If everything is from everywhere, and has to be equally represented, I'll need to find a Monterey Jack cheese maker from West Virginia for our crafts and foodways area."

"I think you'll be able to do it, and you know what you can do with it when you do." (Hangs up.)

There was a young couple from the New York City area. I believe he was the fiddler and she the banjoist, and they were sure that a lack of social connection had prevented their being booked on the National Folk Festival. This was the third time they had applied, and they had come by to argue a point without asking if it was the proper one to argue.

"We don't believe you need a codger connection to play this music well," she said. "I know that some others feel that you have to mess around with those old people, but we can't see how it helps musically."

He was even more explicit: "We just don't think that you need to associate with a bunch of unwashed old geezers to sing and play these tunes. We feel it is a better use of our time to rely on recordings, and people we can relate to in other ways."

I get to be the hero in most of my stories, and this time I really did rise to the occasion. I quoted Hank Williams to them, his dictum that one ". . . . needs to have walked in the row and smelled mule farts to sing hillbilly songs." An uneasy disquiet settled on the room, and they soon excused themselves, citing another appointment. Of course, I'm not absolutely certain that mule farts help a lot, but who am I to argue with Hank?

A few months before his death, Thomas Jefferson (Tommy) Jarrell visited Gambier, Ohio [a college town], to perform a concert. Tommy was feeling his years, and we reminisced about old friends and all-night sessions of some fifteen years before. He said that most people of his age were lonely, but he never had been. The musical visitors still came almost every day, sometimes two or three groups in a single day. "But now, you know who did that?" he said. Then he gave the names, one after the other, a list of the less than a dozen who made him available to all the rest, those who recorded his music and put it in the hands of players everywhere, those who took him west and north to concerts and festivals, those who made his movie, all who gave something important back to this most-generous man. I don't think he forgot anyone. The names ended, and Tommy paused for a moment. "Not a goddamned thing would have happened without them," he said.

The originals of our world of art need the support of do-gooders. Some who were a friend to Tommy may bristle at that term, but I think it a good one. The particular set of do-gooders with whom I am associated amount to a board of 27, 5 employees, and some 300 volunteers. There are no members, no mailing list, not even a statement of purpose beyond what nonprofit incorporation requires. No one in the group is very wealthy or especially famous, and we have no guarantees, no endowment, no certain annual appropriations or grants. But we are organized and committed to each other, there is a reservoir of experience, and some other organizations have faith that our work will be of a high quality.

But Mac is right; we are not interested in doing good for the particular group he is most interested in. We admit to a considerable fondness for them, we wish them good fortune, and consider them fellow travellers and colleagues, but they are not the people we intend to serve with our time or with our lives.

So I will remind him of the devil's greeting to wicked John, who, after years of bedeviling the devil and his little devils, finally dies and staggers up to the gate of hell, looking for a place to stay. The devil grabs a big coal of fire, and flings it over the gate with his greeting: "Here, John, go start a hell of your own somewhere."

The laws of association of our nation enable groups who wish to do almost any kind of good to create a legal cabal for that purpose. So if we're not doing the good that Mac and like-minded people are interested in, it's OK for them to create a hell of their own. It helps to put lots of banjoists on the board. I'd like to assure Mac and the several banjoists on our board of my great admiration for the quiet restraint that all banjoists bring to their art.

# Last Chorus

*Chuck Perdue*

## CHARLES "CHUCK" PERDUE 1930–2010

Noted folklorist Chuck Perdue died at his home in Madison County, Virginia, on February 14, 2010. A professor at the University of Virginia for thirty-six years, Dr. Perdue had led an exciting life.

Born on a cotton farm in Panthersville, Georgia in 1930, Chuck was hammered and instructed by the Great Depression. He never forgot that he came from working people, those often flimflammed by banks, businesses and their own government.

An Army cryptographer during the Korean conflict, he met his wife Nancy in California. Soulmates for fifty-six years, he and Nan had a bright, talented family. She was co-writer of an array of books and articles, and always at his side.

Chuck received a geology degree from Berkeley in 1957. By 1960 he and Nan were in Washington, D.C., Chuck working for the U.S. Geological Survey.

---

From *Sing Out!*, Spring 2010.

There they helped invent a coffeehouse circuit, and began singing folk songs associated with those given to toil. Chuck usually sang lead, and played a vintage Martin guitar. Nan's harmony voice sometimes soared, but she usually held close to Chuck.

They sang at the Ontario Club, and were friends with many bluesmen who also sang there. Chuck helped found the Folksong Society of Greater Washington, still a vital institution.

In 1964, he found John Jackson playing guitar and singing at a Fairfax service station. Chuck got him a gig at the Ontario, many other coffeehouse and festival jobs, and a recording contract, always explaining that he was a friend of the Jackson family, not a manager.

He was elected chairman of the National Folk Festival Association (later renamed National Council for the Traditional Arts). It had run the annual National Folk Festival since 1934, and Chuck and other board members (Andy Wallace, Mike Seeger, Dick Spottswood, John Holum) turned it into a high-quality presentation.

In 1971, Chuck received a Ph.D. in folklore from the University of Pennsylvania. He began teaching at Virginia the same year.

Chuck and Nan fought a long battle to expose the government dispossession of poor people in the Shenandoah National Park. Using the rule of eminent domain, Chamber of Commerce types—among others—hoped to attract tourists to a mountaintop motorway, and forced these old American-stock citizens off the land they had occupied for generations.

The Perdues thought an apology was owed to the descendants. Though they never got one, they told the unvarnished truth in publications documenting this horror.

The Lord will want him at his side, but I suspect Chuck would prefer the land of Torment, so he could chase these jerks a few worlds farther.

# Rediscovering Cambodia's Royal Ballet

*Mark Lynn Ferguson*

Joe Wilson sure wasn't running on sleep when he climbed into a car to be driven to the far side of Thailand at 6:00 a.m.

The prop plane that flew him and a bevy of roots stars—John Jackson, Ricky Skaggs, Jerry Douglas, and Buck White [as well as Buck's daughters: Sharon and Cheryl White]—wobbled to the ground in Bangkok just four hours before. The others enjoyed a three-day break from their globe-hopping tour, one that had already taken them from Honolulu to Hong Kong. But Wilson, then the executive director of the National Council for the Traditional Arts, was on a mission of mercy.

Bouncing along pitted roads, he tried to catch some shut-eye. The ride was too rough, though, and the views too extraordinary—temples resting on stilts, beautiful lakes, and logging camps where elephants moved

---

Excerpted from "Never Be Boring: How a Self-Educated Mountain Man Became a Living Legend," *Smoky Mountain Living*, June/July 2015.

*Author's note: On May 17, 2015, a couple of weeks after this profile of Joe Wilson went to print in the June/July 2015 issue, Wilson passed away. I hope this piece gives you a glimpse of Joe Wilson's wondrous spirit.*

the logs. Each scene reminded Wilson that he was far from home, leaving him to wonder how he'd know if the Cambodian dancers he'd been sent to find were, in fact, the real deal. In his words, he "knew about as much about ancient Asian ballet and music as a hog does about Sunday."

Still, upon learning that Wilson was touring the region, the U.S. State Department had tapped him to visit a group claiming to be Cambodia's Royal Ballet. These were court performers, sponsored by royalty since the ninth century. Now Cambodia's royalty was deposed, and the dancers were on the run. It was 1980, and a brutal regime, the Khmer Rouge, was assassinating Cambodia's intellectuals and artists.

When he rolled into Khao-I-Dang, a sprawling refugee camp on Thailand's border with Cambodia, this country boy—who had read plenty but didn't hold a single degree—may have been the world's least likely emissary. He faced a sea of oxen carts and hungry faces, an overwhelming sight, but stuck to his guns, weaving around blue tarp shelters until he found the dancers.

Despite fleeing their home country and living in abject poverty, they had not given up their art. In a bamboo space with a dirt floor, these performers donned elaborate costumes representing traditional characters—the woman, the man, the giant, and the monkey—and began a stylized routine of tightly disciplined motion, poised legs and elaborate hand gestures refined over 11,000 years.

"This was a scene to test your heart," Wilson told me, remembering their brilliant show thirty-five years later. "A big expert from Washington," he added, sarcastically, "I signed, attesting to their quality."

But that was just the start of what Wilson did for the gifted refugees. The National Council for the Traditional Arts became the dancers' U.S. sponsor, raising funds to support them as they established lives here and booking tours to introduce their breathtaking art form to American audiences.

While the court performers sometimes struggled to make ends meet, relying on charity, they wowed everyone who saw them and, in the end, built international appreciation for what had nearly become a lost art. Even as the Khmer Rouge began to lose control in Cambodia, many of the dancers remained in the States.

"Now," Wilson said, "their children are fine Americans."

# THE CROOKED ROAD

# The Crooked Road

## *Virginia's Heritage Music Trail*

The Crooked Road is a 333-mile stretch of highway, mostly two-lane, that meanders across southwestern Virginia. It connects the Piedmont plateau and the eastern slopes of the Blue Ridge Mountains to the coalfields of the Cumberland Mountains. It also connects some of America's most musical communities.

It has its beginning where the rolling hills of the Virginia Piedmont meet the first range of hazy blue mountains. Beyond are more mountains to the west—wave after wave. Valleys bisect them, and many have a southwest-to-northeast orientation. The Fraser firs and hardwoods atop the high ridges create a look similar to that of southern Canada.

Geography can be a bit twisted here. The road may require twenty miles in order to go ten. Two of Virginia's highest Appalachian peaks are along this road, which crosses tumbling creeks and sedate rivers that have carved deep valleys.

---

Excerpted from the Introduction to *A Guide to the Crooked Road: Virginia's Heritage Music Trail*, copyright 2006 by The Crooked Road: Virginia's Heritage Music Trail, John F. Blair, Publisher; and the tour program book for *Music from the Crooked Road: Mountain Music of Virginia*, National Council for the Traditional Arts, 2010.

A beautiful and oddly misnamed river rises in these mountains near the North Carolina-Virginia border. Called the New River, it is in fact the oldest North American river and one of the oldest on earth. It confounds conventional geography by flowing north, crossing the Great Valley of Virginia and all of mountainous West Virginia before emptying into the Ohio River.

There are other notable streams farther west. The Holston River is a tributary of the Tennessee River, and ultimately of the Mississippi. Virginians at one time floated goods down it to markets in New Orleans. Broad and sedate, the Holston has sweeping curves with mountain backdrops and is prized for floating and fishing. The Russell River, a branch of Kentucky's Big Sandy River, cuts the biggest gorge in eastern America as it escapes Virginia's Sandy Basin near the coalfields.

There are vistas along the Crooked Road so powerful that they become etched in the mind. The beautiful valley of the Breaks of the Russell River—near Clintwood in the coalfields—has a sunset magical and mysterious, like a piece of heaven touching the earth. At the top of every ridge and around every turn of the Crooked Road are sweeping vistas of verdant mountains, invariably mixed with rich shades of blue, scenes that touch the soul. People here often speak of this place as "God's country," and they mean it.

Some places are too beautiful to pass; one must stop and stare awhile. There are small towns with one traffic light, and some with none. There are old mills, places to float the rivers, trails that invite a hike to high places, and even a place where you can bicycle downhill for seventeen miles.

There's a pride in self-sufficiency among mountain farmers here. You'll see huge vegetable gardens at many houses. The heirloom vegetables sometimes sold in roadside stands have rich flavors. Corn, climbing beans, and squash are sometimes planted together—the "three sisters" way of planting originally used here by Indians.

The Crooked Road area has two great resources for instrument making: the Appalachian hardwood forests and the prized tonewood tree. The tonewood is the red spruce, a rare tree that grows along the highest peaks of the mountains. It seems to be an Ice Age survivor. Species with traits similar to it are found in Canada. The "Adirondack spruce" was used for the tops of the now greatly prized pre-World War II Martin guitars. Its rarity led larger makers to turn to other tonewoods, but many luthiers with small shops in this region still seek it out and swear by it.

Friendly people have chosen to make this place their home for generations and keep a historic strand of American music with a fierce devotion that is most unusual in our nation. They keep it with weekly jam sessions in places that are open to all, in festivals that are both community-based and historic, and in small museums and performance venues scattered along the road.

Virginia is one of the places where America invented its music. Of course, historic music is kept in hundreds of other places, but people from the communities along the Crooked Road have had an influence upon the music of their nation that is highly disproportionate to their relatively small numbers.

This music features the old fiddle and banjo sounds that have roots in northern Europe, West Africa, and colonial America. It is a traditional music handed down through generations of Virginians, one richly flavored with ancient ballads and religious music. It has influenced other American music for generations, and still does.

"Taking the crooked road" is a phrase for playing a non-predictable type of fiddle tune. These tunes tend to be among the oldest—those created before ensemble playing became common. These "crooked" tunes may have measures that are inconsistent, portions that are not repeated, or other unusual aspects. They frustrate accompanists, but have a special charm in that they offer unexpected musical twists and turns.

The people and communities along the Crooked Road are as unpredictable as the old crooked tunes. They confound all stereotypes about mountain people and mountain music. They keep many kinds of traditional music, and they keep it well.

## WHY SO MUCH MUSIC HERE?

This question has been asked about southwestern Virginia for almost a century, since its musicians became a major force in the early recording of country music in the 1920s. Thirty-five years later, Alan Lomax, then the nation's most noted collector of roots music, called one small county here "America's richest breeding ground for traditional musicians." But he did not say why.

There are of course good and reasonable answers as to why so many musicians are here, and they reach deeply into Virginia history. But it will be helpful to first consider some of the more recent historic happenings that have drawn attention to this phenomenon.

Thomas Edison created recording technology in the late nineteenth century. That industrial innovation grew apace with other industrialization, especially the cotton mill industry that "went South" from New England after the Civil War. Country musicians who served time in cotton mills include many of the pioneers who invented the style: Fiddlin' John Carson, Henry Whitter, Wade and J. E. Mainer, John W. Rector, the Dixon Brothers, and scores of others.

The first band to record the distinctive Appalachian fiddle and banjo music handed down in Virginia since colonial times was from the coalfields at the western end of the Crooked Road. It was a family string band: the Fiddling Powers Family. The company that recorded the band was astonished by the popularity of the recordings, and other companies took note of it.

The first band to achieve major commercial success in what was to become country music was organized in a Galax barbershop near the beginning of the road. That band was the Hill Billies, and hillbilly music was named for it in much the same way that bluegrass music was named for another band—the Blue Grass Boys—a generation later [see "The Hill Billies: The Band that Named the Music" in *Roots Music in America*].

Famous Victor recording sessions—which music historian Nolan Porterfield called "the big bang of country music"—were held in Bristol. Among those recorded there for the first time were Jimmie Rodgers and the Carter Family, soon to become founding icons of country music. But those Victor sessions also recorded an amazing array of other musicians from an area ranging from the eastern slopes of the Blue Ridge to the coalfields in Virginia's far west.

No one knows how many musicians this area has produced, but there are remarkable statistics from several places. For example, there's the Coal Creek area near Galax. A tiny, narrow road meanders past farms and dwellings, beside a creek, over ridges, and to a low gap in the Blue Ridge. It is a dozen miles in length, and there are no major huddles of houses. But a total of thirty-one bands from along this road have made noteworthy recordings—some in the 1920s for major labels, many since then by independent labels.

The original Carter Family, from near the coalfields at one end of the Crooked Road, greatly influenced the music of the nation by composing and rearranging ballads. Though skilled with banjo and fiddle, the Carters emphasized songs with a guitar lead. Their imprint is indelible.

In the years when the radio dog wagged the recording tail, Carter Family recordings were sold to people who heard them on radio. They were broadcasting from the Mexican border with Texas when the band broke up in 1941. The Carters remain beloved in Southwest Virginia and thousands from around the world annually visit the Carter Fold in Hiltons. It is a great performance hall, as well as a memorial largely built by a dutiful daughter, the late Janette Carter [see "Memories of Janette Carter" in *Roots Music in America*].

Another coalfields family—Carter and Ralph, the Stanley Brothers—brought highly influential ballad-based mountain soulfulness to bluegrass music as it originated. When later bluegrass bands began dabbling in fusion with other musical forms in the early 1970s, the surviving brother, Ralph, created a change of direction with a sound that reached back to the soul-wrenching harmony of the Primitive Baptist Church of his childhood. That ancient sound was an echo of the colonial church. The singing of his mother and father—and his mother's banjo playing—guided Ralph Stanley as he brought much of bluegrass back to its roots.

During the late 1960s and early 1970s, a new wave of hippie and urban musicians and fans from distant places began coming to such events as Ralph Stanley's Memorial Day Festival, the Galax Old Fiddlers' Convention, and similar traditional festivals and contests. Some of the newcomers visited older musicians to learn tunes, enriching two sets of lives.

## RELIGIOUS MUSIC TRADITIONS

There is a common legacy of religious music along Virginia's Crooked Road, a repertoire of songs known by many residents. This is more a cultural legacy than a religious one, with those who have no religious affiliation as well-attuned to the music as those who are believers. These songs reflect relatively recent musical movements, as well as some that go back to colonial times.

The Crooked Road is more than 300 miles long, and its religious music varies according to settlement patterns. The coalfields at the western end have a high concentration of Primitive and Old Regular Baptists, along with Dunkard (German Baptist) singers, who have left their mark even on the secular music of the area. There is more unaccompanied singing here, and religious songs are often "lined out" (the song leader sings a verse that the congregation then repeats). Some historians theorize that lining out originated due to a lack of songbooks; others guess that it accommodated the many who could not read or write.

"Brush arbor" and "county singing" meetings were once common summer activities along much of the Crooked Road. These events brought together people of many faiths. Brush arbor meetings were Sunday afternoon gatherings in small communities, many without a building suitable for a group of singers. So brush was cut as a cover to protect the singers from the sun, and the singing began. County singings were larger gatherings, of a slightly more formal nature, more staged than participatory and often held in the county courthouse auditorium. These are still held in a few counties.

Shape-note musical literacy is still very common along the Crooked Road. This is an older way of noting music, in which the shape of the note tells its pitch. It began in the Philadelphia area in the 1790s, and soon spread to the Shenandoah Valley of Virginia. Shape-note singing schools, usually of two-week duration, are still held in some areas.

## A LIVING TRADITION

The region's musical culture is not all in the past. In fact, there has never been a time when the communities along the Crooked Road were more vigorous in producing stellar musicians.

Consider, for example, the tiny Whitetop community near the summit of Virginia's highest mountain. The Mount Rogers School there has eighty-eight students enrolled in classes from kindergarten to grade thirteen. Some twenty-five years ago, the commonwealth decided that it could not afford a brass band teacher for a school so small, so training in brass band music was dropped. A group of local string band musicians became indignant about this and, with the encouragement and participation of school administrators, began a string band at Mount Rogers School. It was an instant success and inspired similar programs in nearby Virginia and North Carolina. One set of Mount Rogers graduates established a band that toured nationally.

A considerable list could be made of the scores of musicians who have left the area of the Crooked Road to become entertainers in distant places, but the truth is most have not left. Not even Ralph Stanley. He still lives [Ralph Stanley died in 2016] in Dickenson County in the coalfields.

The larger story here is how steadfast the Virginians of this area have been in preferring their homemade music to the fashions and fads of mass-marketed music. Banjoist, fiddler, and singer Dorothy Quesenberry Rorick, of Dugspur, Virginia, put this sentiment in a nutshell: "I just never could think about music as something you buy or sell. It's always a lot better if you make it yourself. It's like homemade biscuits instead of that old loaf bread at the store, or going somewhere instead of looking at pictures of it. So you ought to make your own bread . . . and if you can't pick the banjer, try to marry a banjer picker."

Brilliant Galax fiddler Greg Hooven was only seventeen when he heard the question about why there is so much music in the area. Though he was reared in the Coal Creek community, one of the great music thickets, he had not previously given the matter much consideration. He thought for a moment, then gave an answer so simple as to be profound: "I think it may be because we like music better than football." They clearly do. The Moose Lodge in tiny Galax draws as many as 50,000 people to its Old Fiddlers' Convention. It does so without hiring a single star and with little advertising. An added comment by the genial Hooven clears matters up a bit more: "We're kind of hard-headed. We like our music."

Famous banjoist and fiddler Kyle Creed once lived near Greg Hooven. Creed made some outstanding recordings and traveled to a few festivals in the 1970s. He was invited to more, and to tour clubs across the nation. His thoughts on the matter were caught in an interview: "Music helps you keep your balance. If you work at a sawmill or keep a store, it's good to come home at night and play your instrument. That's better than watching some fool act like he is shooting somebody on the television. It's good for your hands and your head. You can play with your friends on weekends. If you do that, you'll have better hands, a better head, and better friends."

Creed was equally candid in his opinion of professionalism in music: "I have done enough of that to know that it is a hard job. I hear a few people who work at it full time that I like, but I feel sorry for them. They ride along all day, sitting there like a bump on a log, getting sore. They play every night for people they don't know, they're always a long way from their folks, and they get to ride all day again the next day. That's not a good job."

What is clear is that these musicians and hundreds of others from the region do not allow their musical values to be set in Nashville, New York, or Hollywood. To them, music is not a commodity.

Such musicians keep the spirit and values of a place better than its historians. They are participants in a musical community, not spectators, and music is a part of their lives, not an industry controlled from some distant place. Most of these artists make no speeches, but they are the keepers of the true vine.

At the end of the Crooked Road—in Dickenson County, in the coalfields—a fine museum has been built by his neighbors to honor Ralph Stanley's musical contributions. It tells how the sounds of the Primitive Baptists, the ballads of his father, and the banjo playing of his mother are echoed in the sounds of Ralph Stanley. The music Ralph makes is new concert music, but it is imprinted with much Virginia history.

Virginia is justly famous for saving many of the oldest historic sites in the nation. The Virginians who live along the Crooked Road quietly keep their historic strand of living culture, one very much at home in the twenty-first century.

# In Honor of Singers Who Walked through Abingdon

In 1810, when the population of the United States was just over 7 million, as many as 10,000 people a year were walking through Abingdon. A fourth of the people in the United States have an ancestor who passed through during the years when Abingdon was a place where the branch of the Wilderness Road that began in the Yadkin Valley of North Carolina joined the trunk of the Wagon Road that began in Pennsylvania. The Wilderness Road was in use for a century and dwarfs other historic colonial and early American roads in its significance.

Those on this great road to America were seeking land. Some went to Kentucky, and a part of them veered north to Ohio. They filled Indiana and Illinois. They went to Georgia, Alabama, Mississippi, Arkansas, and Texas. They left their mark in Iowa and Missouri. Some died at the Horseshoe Bend, and others at the Alamo. Many women had a dozen or more babies, and these children toiled to build roads, steamboats, and railroads.

---

From the program book distributed at the Abingdon [Virginia] Crooked Road Music Fest, October 5–7, 2012.

There's a well-kept secret about those who walked through Abingdon. They were great singers, and some could play the fiddle and banjo. They laughed with jigs and frolics, wept with laments, and praised their Lord in harmony. Their finest echo is in the mountains around Abingdon.

Many had accents: the musical brogue of the Northern Irish, the throaty rumble of German, and the genial lilt of Huguenots. Some were chained together—slave carrels of men, women, and children sold from the worn-out plantations of Virginia and Maryland to the new cotton lands of Alabama and Mississippi.

Most of the people who walked the Valley Road were too poor to own musical instruments, but they were beautifully trained as singers. They told of old tragedy in solo voices that dipped and soared, made masterful by careful training handed down across generations. Some of their most brilliant modern followers are from near Abingdon: Horton Barker of Marion (1889–1973), Texas Gladden of Saltville (1895–1967), and Elizabeth LaPrelle of Cedar Springs (1989–present).

Mountain churches are built mostly of wood, and the older ones vibrate when voices of faith arise. Some of the greatest in modern times belonged to the Chestnut Grove Quartet, which arose after World War II [see "The Chestnut Grove Quartet: 'We Come from a Place . . . '" in *Roots Music in America*]. They were from the Chestnut Grove Methodist Church in the Moccasin Gap of Clinch Mountain, west of Abingdon, and were heard on Abingdon radio. They played no instruments, but inspired bluegrass bands to sing a cappella, and their sound went around the world. They are all gone now, but before they left, their former teenaged announcer gave a dinner in their honor. His name is Rick Boucher [U.S. Representative for Virginia's 9th Congressional District, 1983 to 2011].

So invite your friends to walk through Abingdon. If they are overcome with a ghostly urge to sing while walking, it will not be the first time it has happened here. The horses, Fanny and Bud, were pulling a big load, so the family walked. The yellow cur dog, ol' Zip, trotted out front.

If you take a late evening stroll after the cars stop, do pause near the old cemetery. Listen carefully. What you want to hear is the jingle of trace chains, the whiffle of a doubletree, the quiet thud of horses' hooves, the creaking of a wagon, perhaps an echo of a sweet voice singing in the distance.

# Genesis of The Crooked Road

I met an intense thinker named Todd Christensen [then Associate Director for the Virginia Department of Housing and Community Development] at a jawboning session in Asheville. The discussion was of Southwest Virginia, its stunning physical beauty, rich history, and especially of its promise for future generations. We were working on museums: Todd on the Ralph Stanley Museum in Clintwood; I was engaged with the Blue Ridge Music Center on the Blue Ridge Parkway.

Todd identified a problem. The counties in the area were small and some were isolated, but they were varied and they did not cooperate with each other. "We need to find something they have in common," he said. I suggested it could be their rich musical traditions, their devoted keeping of strands of our national heritage. We decided to take it to our county-based friends, and to ask them what could and should be done.

Their success and ours has come from a devotion to cooperation and belief in our homes and our neighbors. Together we honor a place and its ways. We are eager to help each other. I live in Grayson County, but

---

From the program book distributed at the Abingdon [Virginia] Crooked Road Music Fest, October 5–7, 2012.

if something good happens in Lee County I am delighted. The volunteers who sit at our table are county officials of many kinds, and lots of ordinary folks. But they have proven themselves extraordinary in what they do.

We are Republicans of many stripes, Democrats of many persuasions, and Independents galore. No one gives a toot about politics. We are for each other, our counties, our traditions, and our place in planning and organizing to help each other. We want a better economy for our people, better education for our children and grandchildren, and a future that continues to love and keep our very special traditions.

Yes, we know that a wish to control the future is the biggest conceit possible. The people who will then be in charge will better know what is best. But we are so conceited about Southwest Virginia that we want them to know we cared enough to keep as much as we could and hand it to them.

# A Statement for The Crooked Road

The Crooked Road has nothing to do with politics. It never has and never will. It is a private group of Virginians who want to create jobs and improve the quality of life in Southwest Virginia.

The Constitution says citizens of the nation can organize themselves in free associations and work on matters that concern them. That's what we are, a free association of volunteers. Some of us are Republicans, Democrats, and independents, and we like each other and share a concern for our region.

We are very optimistic people who believe our region is special and can use its beauty, rich history, and physical resources to create a better future. By "better future" we mean more jobs, better jobs, jobs that can't be exported, and jobs that enhance the nation's appreciation of a very special place.

---

This is a September 2012 public statement in support of the Crooked Road's application for National Heritage Area status, signed "composed for the Crooked Road by Joe Wilson, a co-founder." Later, in March of 2013, the Crooked Road decided that—lacking the unanimous support from all the localities it serves—it would cease pursuit of a National Heritage Area designation.

Does our work have anything to do with property? Yes, it does. We feel it will make all property in Southwest Virginia worth more. We do not apologize for that.

We created our association as a way to get individuals, businesses of many kinds, villages, towns, and counties to work together for the improvement of our area. We do not apologize for that.

We are going to ask the National Park Service to designate our region as a National Heritage Area for two very good reasons. First, it truly is an area that helped shape the nation. It is the place where Campbell gathered the troops that went to King's Mountain and fought a key battle in winning American freedom. The Great Wagon Road is here, literally "the road to America." There are a thousand other historic resources here.

Second, we can obtain some funding for our work with a heritage designation. It would be, at best, about $150,000 a year. We need and would be most grateful for that support. It is nowhere near the preposterous amount our critics estimate.

Our critics jeer even the historic secular and religious music handed down from the ancients in these mountains. We feel this reveals a level of ignorance we should ignore. But what truly amazes us is their assumption that we plan to do some great evil to individual property rights. Nothing could be further from the truth.

We love the Constitution and its amendments. We like the property laws of the commonwealth and those of the common law handed down for many generations. We are traditionalists who believe in self-help, and we believe in each other. We also believe that the people of Southwest Virginia know and understand us.

There is a form of gentle Christianity that was brought here many generations ago by Scots-Irish and German immigrants and their descendants, and it still informs this place. It hears all before it renders judgment. It takes its cues from deeds as well as words. It is unwise to falsely accuse anyone in this place. The accuser is judged along with the accused.

Those who created the Crooked Road believe their neighbors know them well.

# MISCELLANY

# Frog Soup and Blowing Up Powder Houses

## *The Real History of the Blue Ridge Parkway*

Lora Jean Tompkins grew up hearing funny stories about the building of "the Scenic," the name given to the Blue Ridge Parkway by the men who built it.

"The Scenic" was in large measure a make-work project of the Great Depression, supported by President Franklin Roosevelt as a way to create work for many thousands of unemployed mountain farmers. Chambers of Commerce in Virginia and North Carolina had schemed for a generation to create a great park in the East that might rival in economic benefits those in the West, but it was the 1929 crash and disaster of the Depression and the unemployment of a third or more of mountain families that finally persuaded Congress to appropriate funding for it.

The late Haywood Blevins of Baywood told that times were so tough that some people near Independence were then called "frog soupers." "People had always eat frog legs," he said. "But times was so bad they were eating the whole dadgum frog." He had other observations: "If that Depression had lasted a few more years, the groundhog, rabbit, possum, and squirrel would have become endangered species in Grayson County."

---

Found among Joe's files, undated and presumably unpublished.

Mrs. Tompkins' family lived in Grayson County—some five miles north of the Cumberland Knob starting point of the Parkway—and her father, Lester Burcham, was one of the farmers who helped built it. He rode to work every day with his close friend and neighbor, Clark Jennings. Jennings was bold, hardworking, and generous. Mrs. Tompkins recalls that he had rambled out West in earlier years, met Teddy Roosevelt, and had many fine stories.

But her favorite stories were about the building of the Parkway, and the obstacles the neighbors overcame. Jennings then owned an ancient Model T Ford truck, and Burcham and Jennings rode inside while a tangle of neighbors—also employed by the Parkway—rode on the back.

Disaster overtook the truck one day when it was parked near the explosives holding area where black powder and dynamite were kept. The workers called this "the powder house." As Mrs. Tompkins tells it, a fire was set in the dry broomsedge below the house and raced toward it. The building exploded with a great roar but no one was hurt, and the Park Service promised to pay for damages to the workers' property.

There was speculation that a disgruntled former employee had set the fire, but no arrests were ever made. The top was blown off Clark Jennings' Model T, but Henry Ford had made that model of the T so sturdy that it was nearly immortal, so it would still run. The Park Service did not compensate Jennings, possibly reasoning that it did not matter if he and Lester Burcham got wet, as the workers on the back of the truck had been getting wet all along.

According to Mrs. Tompkins, the Park Service did compensate another worker: Onie Andrews. He owned a newer car, a 1928 Model A Ford. Responding to questions, he told that he had paid $17.50 for the car. The Park Service gave him the entire $17.50 value, with the stipulation that he remove the junk. He dragged it home and began finding parts for it. He was able to fix it and drove it for several years. He then sold it for $17.50.

Mrs. Tompkins recalls that Clark Jennings always addressed stories at her house to her father, "By Ned, Lester . . ." He'd begin thusly and the real history of the building of "the Scenic" would be told.

The Brinegar Cabin on the Parkway is a place where Park Service interpreters tell about the foodways and other skills of early settlers.

Caroline Brinegar—who once lived there—is a relative of Mrs. Tompkins, who is bemused to find her life as a child being documented in such fashion.

Like the children of other workers who cut the trees, blasted the rocks, drove the steam shovels, bulldozers, and dump trucks, built the rail fences, and taught the Italian stonemasons to drink moonshine liquor, Mrs. Tompkins has an affection for those who have made the Parkway work for seventy-five years. And her favorite stories about it begin, "By Ned, Lester . . ."

# Reflections on Hogs in Vientiane

You'd have to look long and hard to find a national capital more rag-tag than Vientiane, Laos. We were in one of their best theaters last night with our show, and there were chickens backstage. They were walking around, pecking, pooping, and doing chicken things. It is common to see seven or eight cows walking along a downtown street, hoping to find a patch of grass.

Yesterday, while the U.S. ambassador and I were having a talk on his residence porch, a large hog went strolling past. He didn't say a thing, but I knew he saw the hog. So I didn't say anything either. After all, what are you supposed to say in such circumstances? "Nice hog, Mr. Ambassador. Do you have a lot of them around here?"

That just wouldn't make it. You are supposed to compliment ambassadors about their gardens, their flowers, and their rugs. Of course,

---

From day 30 of Joe's personal journal of a tour of Asia: *From Plains and Pueblos*—Native American music, song and dance of the Zuni of the Southwest and the Lakota of the Great Plains, 1993. The journal was serialized in Joe's hometown newspaper in Mountain City, Tennessee: *The Tomahawk*, where this excerpt was first published on August 11, 1993.

all these things and even their house is actually federal property, and it would make more sense to compliment them about the hogs in their neighborhood, but it just isn't done.

Anyway, I doubt that there is a single ambassador in the entire foreign service that could hold up his side of a talk about hogs. Very few could tell a Duroc from a Hampshire, and I'll bet that fewer than half could tell you when a pig becomes a shoat.

I find it hard to talk to people who don't know anything about hogs. Sometimes when talking to a city dude, I'll toss off a comment about someone being the "runt of the litter" or being "on the hind teat." Usually they just stare at me as if I have lapsed into another language. Our universities teach a lot of silly and arcane subjects, and I think they would be well advised to drop one of them and add a course about hogs, so people could know how to talk.

I'm not sure that it would help our foreign policy if our diplomats knew more about hogs, but the small talk at your average embassy reception makes less sense to me than a rigorous discussion of the finer points of the Poland China breed of swine. A diplomat would think such a breed derived from communism, but it was popular in the 1930s and had reached Trade by the late 1940s.

How did you folks get along for so long without essential information like this?

I've noticed that some people in Johnson County no longer keep up with developments in the hog business, but they tend to be interested in things that are equally useless. A lot of people in the county follow sports and know which team is ahead in which conference. Others spend considerable time eyeballing the blather box in their living room. If a jury of disinterested people could be put together and set to the task of assessing the value of various kinds of information, I'm willing to bet that hog husbandry would beat all sports three to one, and television by twenty to one.

Hey, I've wandered far from the subject. I have you over in Asia with me. I'll get back on the subject.

The cows that wander about in Vientiane all seem to be Guernsey or Jersey. The cream they serve is thick and yellow, the kind that comes from those breeds. I've yet to see a Holstein.

I've seen several herds of goats, and a house across the street from the U.S. Embassy seems to be in use as a turkey roost. Honest—real turkeys, a fowl native to North America. I asked a junior staff member if it was housing for the outgoing Bush staff or the incoming Clinton staff. He didn't laugh. The tropics are tough on people who have no sense of humor. He's liable to crack up or become a stockbroker.

# The King of Kansas

## *A Fable*

Joe Wilson wrote: "This was written in 1988, a letter to my stepdaughter, age eight."

Kathy James, Joe's wife, wrote:

As a little girl, my daughter Jackie loved bedtime stories, and so I would read to her every night. When Joe wasn't working late or on the road, he preferred for them to make up stories together. His alter ego was "Poppa Groundhog," and he would tell her tales about all the animals in the woods where he lived.

Jackie soon had Poppa married to Momma and they had two children: Baby Brother and Baby Sister. After a time, Jackie decided they needed another kid. When Joe asked what they should call this new little groundhog, Jackie said, "Baby Baby." As time passed, the Groundhog family expanded to include twins named Billy and Sarah.

I often regret not hiding a recorder in the room to capture on tape these delightful tales, but—luckily—Poppa once wrote Jackie a letter, and that is how the story that follows was saved. For years, Joe, Jackie, and I held an annual Groundhog's Day party. We would encourage our friends to bring their children, because, at some point during the evening, Joe would gather all the kids around and read aloud Poppa's letter to Jackie. I hope you enjoy it.

A very scary thing happened to the Groundhogs yesterday. They asked me to tell you about it. The little ones had gone over the hill to play, and Poppa was taking a nap when there was a lot of yelling. Suddenly,

Momma burst into Poppa's room. "Oh Lord, Poppa, a very bad boy has caught all our babies and says he is going to cook them and eat them! Oh Poppa, what are we going to do?"

"Where are they?" Poppa asked. "Where did he take them?"

"Up the road by the railroad track," Momma said. "Oh, Poppa, hurry!"

So Poppa ran over the hill and up the road by the railroad track. He saw a big black crow. "Oh, Mister Crow, have you seen Bad Boy with my babies?" he asked.

"Awk, caw, awk," said the Crow. "Awk, caw. Well, yes, Poppa, but you'd better be careful, because he'll catch you and Momma and eat you too, because he eats a lot of small animals, squirrels, groundhogs, rabbits . . ."

"But not MY babies," said Poppa. "Come on, where did he take them?"

Momma had run behind Poppa, and she chimed in, "Yes, yes, tell us. Where did he take them?"

"Well, caw, awk. Over there is the road to the place. Just go around four curves, and look for a house beside a barn with animal skins tacked all over it."

Poppa was gone in a flash, and Momma was right behind him—zip, zip, zip, around the curves, and to the house of the bad boy who ate small animals. The doors were shut and the shades drawn. Poppa saw a tree beside a window. "I'm going to climb that and break a window and get our babies," he told Momma. "Give me a push up the tree."

Momma pushed and soon Poppa was climbing past the first floor to the second floor. "I'm going to sneak in," he whispered down to Momma.

Suddenly there came a voice from above Poppa. "Who? Who? Who?" Poppa stopped and stared up the tree. It was Big Owl.

He replied, "Oh, it's just me—Poppa Groundhog—trying to get my babies back. Can you help?"

"I may be able to," said Owl. "But you have to be very careful or he'll catch you and eat you too."

Poppa was almost too afraid to ask about his babies, but he did. "Has he hurt them?" he asked, his voice full of fear.

"Not yet," Owl said. "His plan is to have Baby Baby for breakfast. Then he'll have Billy and Sarah for a mid-morning snack. Baby Brother will be a BIG lunch. And he intends to have Baby Sister in a groundhog casserole for dinner."

"That gives me some working time," Poppa said. "Where does he have them?"

"That is a problem much too big for you," said Owl. "They are in an all-steel cage you cannot gnaw through. There is a big combination lock on the cage door and two pit bull dogs in front of it. I'm sorry, Poppa, but I think you and Momma should leave. You don't want to watch what is going to happen here tomorrow."

"Oh, horsefeathers!" said Poppa. "No stinking, drip-nosed boy is going to eat my babies! Tell me about this twerp. What does he like? What are his weaknesses?"

Owl thought for a moment. "The only thing he likes more than eating small animals is stories. When he was a little boy, he'd cry when a story was over. Even now he yells when a good story ends. He likes long stories—the longer the better."

Poppa thought about that for a while, then asked, "What window leads to his room?"

"The one just above us," said Owl. "But be careful. He sleeps with his window open."

Poppa climbed up to the window and peeked in. Bad Boy was having a temper tantrum, because a TV show had ended. "More. More!" he yelled. "More. More. More . . ."

"Be patient!" his very ugly mom yelled back. "You're gonna eat groundhogs all day tomorrow, so go to sleep."

"Well, OK," he groused. "But dang it, why are stories so short?"

At that moment, Poppa threw a dry hickory nut from the tree and it hit Bad Boy in the nose.

"Ouch," he said. "Hey, what goes?"

Poppa was flattened out on the other side of the tree. "It's me, the teller of *The Endless Story*."

"Huh?" asked the boy. "Hey, could you tell that one?"

"Not for free," said Poppa. "You have to pay for *The Endless Story*."

"I don't have much," said Bad Boy. "Just some toys I stole, and some stuff I broke, and some little groundhogs I'm going to eat tomorrow. Could we trade?"

"Sure," said Poppa. "I'll tell *The Endless Story*, if you'll let me have the little groundhogs."

"It's a deal," said Bad Boy. "People around here will tell you that I keep my end of a deal, so come out. Let me see you."

When Poppa came around the tree Bad Boy laughed. "Well, look at this, more food." You can't tell a long story, and certainly not an endless one. You've put me on, and I'm going to eat you too."

"That makes you a big liar *and* a deal breaker," said Poppa. "You just said you keep deals. Now you're breaking one. Soon everyone will know."

This made Bad Boy angry. "Why you low-life flea farm!" he began, but he knew Poppa was right. The word that he broke deals would get around.

"OK, Mister Groundhog," he said. "I'm calling your bluff. You said you knew an endless story, and I said I would turn the little groundhogs over to you after you told it. So tell your story, but when it ends you are in BIG trouble. I'm going to put you into the cage and fatten you up and feed you to my pit bulls."

"Fine," said Poppa. "Here's your story."

"Once they had a king in Kansas, and he kept all the wheat. It is a big state, and you can drive for hundreds of miles beside wheat fields with billions of bushels of wheat. The king kept all the wheat in huge grain elevators in the middle of the state. You could drive for an hour beside the grain elevators. One day, the first mouse came to Kansas.

"He gnawed a hole into one corner of the grain elevator at the end of all the elevators. He got one grain of wheat and carried it across the road, then he came back and got another grain of wheat and carried it across the road. Then he came back and got another grain and carried it across the road. Then he came back and got another grain and carried it across the road. Then he came back and got another grain and carried it across the road . . ."

"Hey, would you get on with the story," Bad Boy interrupted. "This stuff about carrying grains across the road is boring. You sound like a stuck record."

"But that is the story," Poppa said. "The mouse has to carry all that wheat, grain by grain, which is what makes the story endless, so I'll go on with it. Then he came back and got another grain and carried it across the road . . ."

"Would you shut up!" yelled Bad Boy. "I don't like this story. You are hung up on one part."

"But it is a true story," said Poppa, "and I have to tell all of it, and our deal was that you would listen. So here goes. Then he came back and got another grain and carried it across the road . . ."

"Hold it. Hold it!" said Bad Boy. "How long does this part go on, this carrying of one grain of wheat?"

"A very long time," said Poppa. "I'm sure it will take many years, and you will have to learn to be patient. He has only carried eight grains across the road so far, so I'd better get on with it. Then he came back and got another grain and carried it across the road. Then he came back and got another grain and carried it across the road . . ."

"OK, that's ten grains, " said Bad Boy. "How many are left?

"Billions and billions, " said Poppa. "You see, this one little mouse has to carry all the wheat in Kansas across this wide road. So, then he came back and got another grain and carried it across the road . . ."

"Shut up!" screamed Bad Boy. "You are driving me crazy with this one-grain mouse. The deal is done."

"OK," said Poppa. "But the deal was that I get the little groundhogs, and I'm not going to stop until you bring them. So, then he came back and got another grain, and carried it across the road . . ."

"Enough! Enough!" yelled Bad Boy, pulling Billy, Sarah, Baby Baby, Baby Brother, and Baby Sister out of the cage and putting them on the windowsill.

"OK, Sarah, you're first," said Poppa. And she jumped into his arms. Poppa dropped her to Momma waiting below. All the others followed, as Poppa kept a fixed stare into the eyes of the bad boy, ready to have that mouse go get another grain if he so much as moved. Then Poppa dropped from the tree and they ran home.

That night Poppa tucked the babies in. "Would you like to hear a story?" he asked.

"Uh-huh." Said Billy and Sarah. "Oh yes," said Baby Baby. "Sounds great," said Baby Brother. "You betcha," said Baby Sister.

"OK," said Poppa. "Then he came back and got another grain and carried it across the road . . ."

The baby groundhogs seldom say anything all together, but this time they did. "Be quiet, Poppa!" they yelled.

Downstairs, Momma giggled and hugged Poppa. "You're so mean," she said. But you could tell that she really liked Poppa.

The End

# Joe's Gems

## *A Compilation of Eloquent and Memorable Short Communications*

Here are memorable fragments from Joe Wilson's e-mails, letters, testimony, and posts to the Publore listserv for the public folklore community, which Joe, his friends, and associates thought deserved to be anthologized.

Joe's wife, Kathy James, wrote: "Among the folks who knew Joe, all would agree that he was never at a loss for words. Those finding themselves on the opposite (WRONG) side of an argument with him were often taken aback by his quick-witted, acerbic, and usually humorous comebacks. Joe's way with words seemed to come naturally, but his library contained well-worn volumes by H.L. Mencken and Nancy McPhee's *The Book of Insults, Ancient and Modern: An Amiable History of Insult, Invective, Imprecation and Incivility (Literary, Political, and Historical).* For him, the art of word play held the same wisdom as the old joke, 'How do you get to Carnegie Hall? Practice, practice, practice!'"

Crooked Road executive director Jack Hinshelwood wrote: "Joe is a lover of, and has an extraordinary and entertaining command of, the English language, both written and spoken. Like the old E.F. Hutton commercials, 'When Joe Wilson speaks, people listen.' His love of language and wonderful sense of humor are exhibited in these excerpts."

### KISSED BY MOTHER MAYBELLE

From a December 29, 1987, letter of thanks to Jan Arnow, who had sent Joe a copy of her book, *By Southern Hands: A Celebration of Craft Traditions in the South* (Oxmoor Press, 1987).

Dear Jan:

Winter has come to the high part of the Blue Ridge. It is ten degrees outside and the wind is blowing lonesome. It whistles and wails as it crosses the Wilson farm on Bulldog Creek. The snowfall stopped before dark, but blowing snow makes everything white beyond the living room window. There's a loose board on the old barn that creaks as it is pulled and pushed by the wind. I could fix it tomorrow with two nails and six licks with the hammer, but, so far, I like it. Barn and house creaks need to be aged and enjoyed. I can enjoy one for two or three weeks. Then, one day, I'll have had as much of that goddamn creak as I can stand. It'll have to be fixed at that instant, and if I were serving as pallbearer, I'd drop the coffin and go get the hammer and nails.

But tonight I like the creak, and there's a good red oak fire in the heater. For supper Mama fixed Shelley beans, cooked apples, creasy greens, and white flint cornbread in an iron skillet. Then she went to bed early, as she has for most of her seventy years. I washed the dishes and then dug out the old Martin guitar and sang a few just for the hell of it.

I thought Mama was asleep until she called down a request for "The Wildwood Flower." For as long as I can remember, "The Wildwood Flower" has been the favorite song of almost everyone around here, and not just their favorite Carter Family song. My guitar-making friend Wayne Henderson believes they think it is the national anthem, the song others are measured by. My musical skills are damn near nil, but mothers are awfully forgiving, so I did it for her. My reward was, "Thank you. Now you'd better get to bed because I'm going to get you up in the morning." Go to bed at 8:30 p.m.? Jan, the guy that looks back at me from the mirror nowadays is a city dude.

In the early 1940s, the Carter Family played at the old Sutherland school near here in Ashe County, North Carolina. My mama is a Sutherland, and we then lived near the school. She took my older brother and me to the concert. She recalls that Maybelle "picked up one of the boys and carried him around and kissed him. . . . ." By the time I got to Nashville in the late 1950s, I'd heard that story many times. So backstage one night at the Grand Ole Opry, I told Maybelle that we'd met before, and that I'd been concerned that it may have been my brother Kenneth who got carried around and kissed.

She came right over and sat in my lap and kissed me and said, "Now you can quit being jealous of your brother!"

## LETTER TO A CRITIC

Joe Wilson wrote: "Producers of festivals, tours, recordings, and films are often severely criticized. I seldom had time to argue, so I borrowed a response from H. L. Mencken, who had adapted it from Mark Twain: "Dear Sir: You may be right." I had another for those especially rude: "Dear Sir: Some idiot has sent me a letter and signed your name to it. A copy is enclosed." But occasionally I had a bit of time. This response to a rude letter was written during the years when some in Congress wished to end all public support for the arts. It was sent to a critic of the Native American tour featuring music and dance from the Zuni, Lakota, Eskimo, Cherokee, and more."

November 21, 1994

Dear Mr.———:

I'm sorry you didn't like *From Plains, Pueblos and Tundra*.

Given the mood of the country and the very gloomy fiscal prospects of organizations like ours—as well as those of the Arts Endowment—you need not worry about there being a future oversupply of traveling shows from the terribly crude American grassroots.

You've made me feel like the captain of the Titanic, receiving a complaint about the quality of the finger foods on the shuffleboard court.

You may wish to lay in a supply of colorized Ginger Rogers and Fred Astaire movies.

And the best of luck to you.

Sincerely yours.
Joseph Wilson
Director

## WEENIE-WAVING AND WEEVILISM

Posted to Publore: December 1, 1997.

[Recent posters to this listserv] are not in full agreement about what I meant in some parable that jumped out of this machine, so I will bless them and Publore with another visitation concerned with The Meaning of Life.

I've been called by a lot of hypemeisters during the last forty years who wished to influence my work. I never ask if the hypemeister on the line is an artist, folklorist, Rosicrucian, or moonlighting Roto-Rooter operator. What I know is that they have called me.

Our operation [the National Council for Traditional Arts] has some altruistic and folkloric values, and it needs to survive. The people who work for it tend to be passionate about arts developed by the sweat-stained. That's a poor definition, but all the definitions are poor.

[A person who posted to the listserv] seems to feel that some deeply traditional people sell themselves in the arts marketplace. My experience is that a few do, but it is relatively rare. Among the scores of truly great artists we have presented over the years—some for the first time on a big stage—there is not one who called us.

We deal with artists we find through the recommendations of people we trust, and our own fieldwork. Some are highly commercial. Alison Krauss performed at our festivals and on a national tour at age fifteen, before she had a distributed recording. She had no agent and didn't call. I saw her at a little local festival and talked to her mom. Quality was the attraction.

I can't recall anyone here ever asking whether or not Alison or anyone else is "commercial." That form of discussion is food for Marxists, squirrels, and other head-trippers insulated from the realities of the workaday world they purport to understand and represent.

If our process needs a label, let's give it an aesthetic one. The instrument is in tune or out, and we prefer in. The lick is hit or missed, and the rhythm is on or off; the performance works or doesn't. And like most other devotees of the arts, we prefer originals to copies.

I have on my desk a promo package from a Hank Williams wannabe. He has posed himself like Hank in the brown Western-cut suit photo. Hank was pencil-thin and forever young in that photo, fingering a "C" chord on the Martin, his eyes fixed on some distant Nirvana seen only by those who inject the essence of the poppy plant.

The wannabe has the suit, microphone, Martin, and "C" chord, and I'd bet my front seat in hell he gets close to Hank's intonation. But he is older, a bit pudgy, and the glint in his eye is that of a wharf rat eyeing an ear of corn. I'd bet that he has an exercise machine and is devoted to designer water. I'm gonna put his whole goddamn package into the round file.

Is this fair? No. That is not in my job description. I saw Hank when I was a kid and I'm not buying any copies of him, nor any copies of European Masters from the Art Collector's Guild now showing up in my spam.

I'm sympathetic if a hard-working recreation director has forty kids beset by pubescence and hyperactivity in a clogging class, and wishes to discipline them by getting them to aim at a performance at a really big festival.

But I may have bigger problems. I served awhile as one of two persons organizing three festivals and two tours annually, the mail being delivered daily in a medium-size mail sack, eleven phone calls an hour, and three calls a day from clogging teams. During that time, a clogging hypemeister could not persuade me to engage in a long discussion of the meaning of clogging tradition.

Is dance now done to recordings? Sure. Has this gone on since the 1920s? Sure. Is it still traditional? I don't care. What I know is that I don't put it on stage. Does that mean that I have caught the Artistic Director Disease? Maybe. But I've seen a lot of it, and in my view such dance comes up as short as John Bobbitt at a weenie-waving, and I say to hell with it.

Can we change the subject of this discussion to something interesting, like the effect of the pink bollworm on the direction of American arts?

He persuaded Rose Maddox's family to ride boxcars from the Sand Mountain plateau in Alabama to California, and become fruit-picking tramps and barroom performers. He got the Delmore Brothers to flee the same area of Alabama and wander among the nation's radio stations.

He sent a hundred times more black folk to Chicago than Moses led to the Promised Land. He made Vernon Presley move from Mississippi to Memphis, where Elvis heard and liked R&B, country, and gospel. I say that little pink bastard defined the direction of American art.

Yes, I know they have a statue honoring him in southern Alabama. But that is not enough. We need a scholarly book that belabors the culture and economics that made weevilism possible.

## STROLLING TOWARD CHATTANOOGA

This is a note to Dalton Roberts (1933–2015) sent April 23, 2004. Joe Wilson wrote: "Dalton is a former county executive of Hamilton County (Chattanooga) and a songwriter of great merit."

Andy Wallace, Joe's former associate at NCTA, wrote: "Dalton and Joe were good friends, peas in a pod in some ways. Dalton was instrumental in smoothing the way during the National Festival's sometimes rocky three years in Chattanooga. He was a fine writer himself, and a good musician to boot. He played at the festival one year with his band, as I recall." Ellipses replace colorful profanity.

Dalton,

This morning I killed a large green fly with the little guitar-shaped swatter you gave me. This is the one that has your name and essential information on it. I'd been using it as a fan, but it was rather ineffective in that role. But this morning, a large and very hairy green fly flew in my window and landed on an expensive brochure extolling tourism in Tennessee.

He was of the iridescent green type. . . . He looked at me with one large brown eye, rubbing his front legs together over his head in the manner of George W. Bush greeting the Polish people.

He then rubbed his hind legs together, taking a forward bow, seeming to say, " . . . Buford, I'm taking over." . . . I reached for the fine little swatter you bestowed upon me. The fly was strolling toward Chattanooga on the image of Tennessee on the brochure as I drew back. He jumped . . . as I swung down, but I got him.

He rolled over and wiggled his legs as he departed this vale of tears. I noticed a stenciled logo on his side, "ET&WNC." He is the first fly I have seen exploiting his intellectual property possibilities, and I wish I had interviewed him before swatting him. I'm sure I could have gotten more than a buzz out of him about brand exploitation.

And it was good to see the ET&WNC logo is still out there. It was used by a Johnson City transportation company in my youth, and we thought all the big trucks on earth belonged to them. We may have known that the acronym was for Eastern Tennessee and Western North Carolina, but we told visitors it was for "eat taters and wear no clothes" and tried to get them to go snipe hunting.

I hope your health is progressing well, and that you have taken up with some young hussy. It probably won't work out, but you will get lifted up before you fall. I thought you would want to know about the fly, and would welcome my counsel on your love life.

Joe

## WILSON'S RODENT STUDIES

Joe Wilson wrote: "Jay and Derrick are good friends who had ties to *Blue Ridge Backroads*, aired on Friday night on WBRF in Galax, Virginia. In 2010 they cut off a live broadcast from Galax's Rex Theater by rockabilly ace Bill Kirchen. I sent this protest to them and shared it with many others via handbill."

Derrick and Jay,

I was taken aback when I learned that you bopped Bill Kirchen off the WBRF air a few minutes into his program. . . . No one in my hearing range has said *Blue Ridge Backroads* is devoted solely to bluegrass and old-time country. But, if it is, kicking Bill off in the midst of a show is awfully rude.

. . . . You guys should know that your joint exercise in censorship irked some regular station listeners and I have heard from them. I won't burden you with the more vitriolic messages, but I am enclosing a sample, one sent to the Galax Chamber of Commerce. . . . I don't know him. He is your listener, and you may want to respond to him.

But I feel he overstates the case in comparing you to Hitler and Stalin. You are indeed self-appointed censors, but he clearly overstates the situation. If you were comparable, which of you would be which? I can see the two of you as Laurel and Hardy or even as Lonzo and Oscar—but not as Homer and Jethro. They had class.

. . . . Of course Bill K. learned about his on-air insult by Jay from fans that follow his website and heard the broadcast. He was initially puzzled. "D'ya think I was not using the Lester Flatt G-run enough?" he asked.

I could hardly sleep for three days after this happened. Why on earth did Jay and Derrick want to insult their friend and diss a nice guy like Kirchen? It became obvious that the idea had to originate with someone else, but I could not figure out who that was. Then last night as I was about to nod off, it came to me in a flash. I sat bolt upright and yelled the name—Mickey Mouse!

This is clearly a Mickey Mouse game, and is redolent of his tactics. There was this scurrying about before the concert, but nothing said. . . . Given that you guys have joined up with Mickey, I've tried to locate Mickey Mouse hats for you, but have so far been unsuccessful. So I called my daughter, who is a world-class cartoonist, and asked if she could render the two of you in Mickey Mouse gear: "I want them in little balloon britches with their tails sticking out and in black clodhopper shoes, just like Mickey wears."

"Dad, do you have photos of these guys," she interrupts. I had to confess that I do not. So can I persuade you guys to get photographed together so I can go forward with this? If you will provide this photo, I will have her insert between you—also wearing Mouse togs—the most famous censor of all time, Tomas de Torquemada, Inquisitor General of Spain during the Inquisition. Old Tomas fried 'em by the thousands, so I know he would happily help you put 'em off the air.

As soon as I have Laurie's rendering of the Three Censorship Mouseketeers, I will write an appropriate opus honoring your work in keeping the airwaves pure and pristine, and submit it and the drawing to the *Galax Gazette*. If the *Gazette* declines it as editorial material, I will purchase space for it. I only want you to get what you deserve. . . .

## BASHING THE SELF-APPOINTED SCOURGES OF PUBLIC FOLKLORE

Posted to *Publore* listserv: July 11, 2011.

[In a post from a few years back, concerning a book that had criticized public folklore] I was rapped for biting too hard (note the mixed metaphor). I retaliated in the proper way, which is by pontificating—as follows:

Huh? I can't bash the self-appointed scourges of public folklore anymore? And do I have to also give up bashing politicians, agency heads, college presidents, coaches, players, and left-lane drivers? If so, could I have some time at a halfway house before I totally quit?

If I laugh occasionally, it is not because of a lack of respect. I've spent much of my life in the company of pedagogues and practitioners in cultural studies and folklore, and the emotion I feel most often for them is affection. I giggle because the academic and public sides of folklore remind me of Laurel and Hardy. Folklore's attempts to gain acceptance in state arts agencies and in academia echo Stan and Ollie's work in delivering the piano.

When one of our ideological colleagues mounts the soapbox and berates the pea beside him in the pod for some flaw in the status of folklore, I understand that he is delivering a piano. He has morphed into Ollie, yelling and gesticulating to an oblivious world with one hand, while the other wags an accusing finger under the nose of Stan—his only friend. Laughter is a good antidote to the self-absorption that poisons and blinds perspective.

San Francisco longshoreman and thinker Eric Hoffer observed that those who could claim least credit for themselves were often the first to claim all credit for their race or nation. He could have added profession. An obsessive concern for the status of his profession—intellectual and otherwise—marks the eternal sophomore in the workforce.

There's an enormous backlog of cultural work to be done in communities across our nation. We have the concern, training, and experience to do important parts of it. If we do this work, the communities and country will take care of us.

But I'm not going to unilaterally disarm. I feel it is reasonable and responsible to inquire about any contributions to human welfare made by the more acerbic critics of our discipline. Having a gimlet eye and ratchet jaw is certainly a contribution, but of a minor sort. I'll need to hear about ships they've launched and worlds they discovered.

## LOUD-MOUTHED BOTHERSOME ROOT SUCKERS

Jack Hinshelwood said about this 2012 e-mail, "When opponents sent out a diatribe against the Dan River Association's plan to preserve a section of the river, one of our Crooked Road board members was concerned about their efforts. Joe was not as concerned, and wrote this to that board member."

I saw your complaint about these mouthy ones, and it is clear you have not yet been briefed about who they are, what they do, and their lifecycle.

I feel it is my duty to help you with this before their increasing noise persuades you to seek the solitude of the Rocky Mountains.

They are a part of the cycle of the cicada, a parasitic insect that spends seventeen years underground, sucking on a hardwood root. This is, of course, a violation of the property rights of the hardwood and its owner, a tax-paying citizen of the commonwealth. Some of the larger cicadas have red eyes, and though they are big and bumbling and among the larger insects, have a brain smaller than that of a gnat. I'm sure you know some of their relatives: the leaf hopper, the spittle bug, and jumping plant lice. Their seventeen-year coming is a boon to their animal fans, including rats, mice, and scavenger birds. Vultures are among these at the height of the season. These creatures are especially annoying because of their noise, a high-pitched screeching reproductive call that can last five days. (It might be good if your supervisors passed a ban on five-day reproductive screeching in Scott County.) Finally, these are merely loud-mouthed bothersome root suckers, and no one should expect anything positive from their bumbling across our path.

I am happy to have cleared this up for you. Feel free to post it in the hall or speak it on the radio. With my best,

Joe

## BOOGER MAN-DIS RUN AMOK

E-mail from Joe Wilson to Jack Hinshelwood, October 7, 2012, responding to an e-mail received from an opponent to a National Heritage Area designation for the Crooked Road.

Jack,

This is what I would have said had I been at that meeting:

I stopped believing in the Booger Man a long time ago. I want to say that twice: I don't believe in the Booger Man, and fear of what we are doing is no more logical than another Booger Man tale. To say that we, or the Park Service, or anyone involved with this wants to become (and I quote) "an ultimate authority" is to raise up a big old imaginary Booger Man, one with lots of hair, that makes big noises, and that smells bad. It just isn't true.

. . . . Making anything the government does a Booger Man is not very helpful, either. With all things that are living and moving, there is the possibility of doing good. Sometimes it may not turn out good, but there is always the possibility of fixing it. To hunker down and do nothing is the worst possible thing to do.

In our little organization of cooperating friends, we talk about what is good, and how we can make it happen here in our communities. If we thought something bad was upon us that we could stop, we would. But we are realists, and we know the day only has twenty-four hours, and not the forty or more you need to deal with vapors about Booger Men.

Yes, we do think a little more planning by everybody might be helpful. Fewer people would be broke or in jail. They might save more money, build better towns, join civic organizations, perhaps start a Sunday school. But we don't intend to take anyone's back yard or front yard, or even their hula hoop. We are givers, not takers. We've never grabbed anything and to charge us with that is Booger Man-dis run amok.

. . . . Does anyone really believe that some agency of the government has some big plan to get control of communities by saying it has an exemplary heritage, and that its heritage should be recognized? There are terms for that kind of thinking: "demonizing" is a good one. People who assume the devil is coming to carry them off in a gunny sack are still around, and we have to sympathize with them. I think we also need to pray for them, because they have left reality back there in Booger Man Land with all the other fanciful illusions that trouble life. It is a form of dysfunction bordering on a mental handicap now manifesting itself as politics, and it is befuddled, bedraggled, bemused, and begs to be ignored. . . .

## HISTORY FOR SALE

Joe Wilson wrote: "This is a letter sent to the editor of the *Montgomery County* [Maryland] *Journal* in 2013. I was visiting my daughter and her family in Damascus, Maryland, and left for home the next day. Was it published? Beats me."

A small colonial structure stands neatly and grimly against a blue sky on the bank of Mullinex Mill Road near its junction with Long Necker Road, near Damascus in Montgomery County, Maryland. Steep-roofed and windowless, its logs are chinked with stones and mud, and the dark interior is blackened by the smoke of two and a half centuries. Nothing could have lived in this ancient working structure; it is clearly the detritus of an ancient industry.

The real estate sign that proclaims it for sale seems utterly incongruous. This is ancient landscape, a part of Maryland history. How could it be for sale?

It is a tobacco house, and there was a time—around 1650—when such little houses dominated the landscapes of Maryland. The name "tobacco house," rather than "tobacco barn," tells that it is of early colonial origin.

It was tobacco cultivation that brought so many indentured servants to Maryland during the generations before the American Revolution. Lord Calvert had recommended mixed agriculture, but tobacco was a cash crop that created a rush comparable to gold and petroleum for later generations. Wood fires helped speed the tobacco drying. Building smaller structures helped lessen the fire hazard; a planter might occasionally lose a house, but not the entire crop in a large barn.

Erected by semi-skilled indentured servants and slaves, houses like the one on Mullinex Road had a single door, one just large enough for a large hogshead barrel of tobacco to be rolled out. Before the rolling, the hogshead was "prized" (packed) full of the yellow-red leaf. It was flipped onto its side and rolled, horses or mules pulling an apparatus attached to each end of the hogshead. Thousands of these large barrels once grumbled along Long Necker Road toward schooner landings on the Patuxent River. The vessels that came during the winter and spring "freshing" of the river carried the crop to markets in London or Amsterdam.

Just this one tobacco house is left where thousands once stood, and it is one too many. We know this is so because the Montgomery County Council, with the pecksniffing delicacy of a bevy of dowagers discerning roasted groundhog, has said, in effect, that it is worthless.

Of course this message was cloaked in the bureaucratic blather of the pronouncements of preservation, and one esteemed council member expressed the faint hope that someone might save it, but not with public funds—praise God.

Maryland was built by working people, and with a commitment to justice that eluded many other colonies. But over the years its commitment to preservation, in the hands of this Council, has left the realm of ideas and gone off in the direction of gingerbread mansions.

The ancient tobacco farm on Mullinex Road has been sold and flipped, and the real estate developers are panting to build rows of identical apartment houses. They will be stacked, of course, and the distances between them measured in quarter inches. Despite the promises of these posh merchants of country living, they will not last as long as the little tobacco house. Within a century, their selfsameness will be declared a pestilence and they will be obliterated by means not yet discovered.

Can we do anything? We can certainly hope for better planning from the Council. Maryland's tiny handful of monuments to ancestors who sweated, swatted, and built freedom should be honored.

Joe Wilson
Damascus, Maryland

## SELF-APPOINTED NUDGE

September 6, 2013, e-mail to Ken Landreth, a collaborator with Joe on the Blue Ridge Music Center. Landreth has since retired and moved home to Fries, Virginia, where Joe lived for the last decade of his life.

I appear before you in my self appointed role of nudge. There's a fine book to be made of Blue Ridge musical instrument makers. It needs to be one of defining photography and thoughtful reflection. It demands context and solid historical facts, and a text that reaches out and ensnares. It needs heart as well as soul.

It would need Stephen Landreth, his tools, and his instruments; Jimmie Edmonds, his father Rush, and one or more of his instruments; Roscoe Russell and his Melton forbears and those instruments; Wayne and Jayne Henderson and items made by Wayne's mom; and the great time-defining photo of Walt Henderson and Bailey Richardson on the porch of the store in front of the Rugby Post Office; Kyle Creed and those who learned from him—the list goes on and on.

There is the opportunity to tell what it means. Wayne used to take every instrument to Albert Hash when it was finished, and bask in his praise. Albert is gone, but Wayne told me he still takes every instrument to him in his imagination: "I know what he would say, and I can hear it." A story by Albert would fit here, perhaps the one about his first fiddle. We weep at his grave, but we also hear his voice.

This requires photos that are world class. Jon Lohman might lend us the lad working for Virginia Humanities. But it mainly requires focus and commitment from Ken.

I am your nudge, and I am on your ass.

Joe

## EVICTION OF THE FESTIVAL

Joe Wilson wrote: "This was submitted to the interior subcommittee of the Senate Appropriations Committee in 2014 as written testimony concerning use of the National Mall, nominally under the control of the National Park Service. The NPS has long wished to evict the Smithsonian Institution's Festival of American Folklife from the Mall due to its golf course mentality about the appearance of the Mall."

I respectfully address these comments to the subcommittee responsible for the overall budget of the National Park Service.

I ask that the subcommittee reject the budget of the Park Service. The NPS seems bent on changing the function of the National Mall. The rules it sets forth for National Mall use would convert the Mall use into a grass-growing enterprise. If growing better grass is the intent of the Congress, the subcommittee would be better served, at much lower cost, by seeking a contract with a contractor devoted to the use of Scott's Turf Builder grass seed and chemicals and golf puttering.

The National Mall is our version of Tahrir Square in Cairo and Tiananmen Square in Beijing. Our concept of modern demands for democracy is imprinted with a vision of an anonymous Chinese fellow standing in front of a tank. Our historic vision should be imprinted with a vision of the Grand Army of the Republic on parade in 1865, after ensuring that the greatest threat the nation has ever faced was defeated, slavery ended, and a great nation emerging.

The Smithsonian Folklife Festival has been a window on the people of the nation for forty-seven years. It has been the place where adobe makers and snow house keepers could show their art. It has been the place where the Zuni could sing the "Sunrise Song" in honor of their nation. It has been the place where Appalachian people can sing the ancient hymns that have sustained them. It has been the place where a slogan such as "out of many, one" could be given meaning.

The National Park Service wears a Spanish American War costume because it was taken out of the U.S. Army shortly after that conflict. It has gone about its galvanization of the National Mall with all of the aplomb of Roosevelt chasing Spaniards off San Juan Hill. It has accepted no compromises and conducted itself as if it is seeking revenge for the sinking of the Maine.

When the late Sidney Yates was chairman of this subcommittee, he fiercely resisted the Park Service accepting gingerbread mansions for keeping, the construction of more visitor centers, and major grounds-keeping duties. He firmly believed that those who seek wilderness should find it, and did not need a guide at every turn. The vision of mounted roly-poly rangers chasing youngsters who drop gum wrappers on the grassy Mall would leave the late chairman agog.

I feel the nation is blessed by those ordinary citizens who fight its wars and haul its garbage. If they wish to show their art, they should be welcomed. If some grass is damaged, it is a small price for honoring our freedom. Thank you.

## COMMON CAUSE IN THE WILDERNESS

Posted to *Publore*: February 18, 2015.

Most study of the Underground Railroad focuses on the years immediately preceding the Civil War. But slavery and the struggle against it were part of the nation's history for more than 200 years. Did the yen for freedom reach a fever pitch shortly before that conflagration? Perhaps, but there are other explanations, and folklorists have studied them. A major one is the runaway who took refuge in the nearby wilderness, and made common cause with others finding safety there.

Folklorist William Cohen wrote a fine book about the Jackson Whites, a mixed-race group that found refuge in the Ramapo Mountains, west of New York City. Though his findings were wonderfully detailed, the relatives of those who hid from the opprobrium of the tar brush did not accept them.

I come from one of the several areas where "Melungeon" is a term attached to folks claiming Portuguese ancestry. Their origin story is a flimsy fiction but has existed for two centuries.

There are other groups who carry a delightful Bureau of Ethnography term: "tri-racial isolates" (the term applies to ancestry claims, usually Indian and white, but invariably black). They are spread across the nation, and these groups offer a rich mining ground for those fascinated by the deeper and less generalized history of the nation. I'm researching one at the moment: a Tennessee group, part of the earliest migration that prospered and is now largely understood to be white. This facet of our history gleams richly into folklore.

["Gleams richly into folklore" seems an appropriate phrase to end this compilation. Joe Wilson died three months after it was written, on May 17, 2015.]

# INDEX